Shifting the Lens in History Education

Shifting the Lens in History Education

Centering Racial and Ethnic Knowledge in the Classroom

MARIBEL SANTIAGO
TADASHI DOZONO

HARVARD EDUCATION PRESS
CAMBRIDGE, MASSACHUSETTS

Paperback ISBN 9781682539644
Library of Congress Cataloging-in-Publication Data is on file.

Published by Harvard Education Press,
an imprint of the Harvard Education Publishing Group

Harvard Education Press
8 Story Street
Cambridge, MA 02138

Cover Design: Patrick Ciano
Cover Image: "The first one is pronounced chee, the second one is eks" (2023) by Melanie Cervantes

The typefaces in this book are Adobe Garamond Pro and Myriad Pro.

Contents

Foreword

I walked into Ms. Navarro's classroom on the first day of school as an eager second grader. I was a student at an elementary school in the heart of the Puerto Rican community in Chicago. I remember Ms. Navarro taking us on fieldtrips all over the city, and although not technically an ESL classroom, we were never silenced for speaking in Spanish. Although it had only been a few years since I had migrated from Puerto Rico, to a seven-year-old, the warmth of home felt like a distant memory. Ms. Navarro, herself a migrant from Puerto Rico, did not want us to forget home. Even if there was no room in the prescribed curriculum, we spoke of it; she memorized the names of our towns across the archipelago, received funding so we could attend the annual Puerto Rican Day Parade, and walked us through our neighborhood streets to see the beautiful murals adorning buildings. Our city and its streets were our classroom. Our stories were used to support our literacy. Our teacher saw us. As a child I saw the possibility of learning, even if in just one classroom. Those are lessons I have never forgotten, even when I never heard the word "Puerto Rico" spoken by other teachers in the countless classrooms I would subsequently enter. For the three years I spent with Ms. Navarro, who I was as a Puerto Rican child was affirmed every day. I fell in love with teaching and learning because of those very lessons she taught me. Lessons I hope to pass on to my own students. As many have come to learn, the question I always ask them when I meet them for the first time is, "Tell me about home?" Home. Not just the structure you reside in but home, the places, stories, and people who reside in you. Our stories matter.

The novelist Thomas King reminds us of "the truth about stories, sometimes that's all we are."[1] Stories allow us a way to position the past as a bridge to the future. Stories, especially for racialized, minoritized communities, are sometimes all that remains of us within a settler colonial context. Stories can and should be pedagogical tools to allow us to imagine more. Yet, our classrooms often become spaces where erasure is reinforced, embedded in teaching practices and curricula that decenter the very lives present within schools. Our communities, especially our community children, deserve more. This is what reimaging the work and practices of teaching history should do: provide not just a narrative of lived experiences, although important, but also provide a deeper and more nuanced account of the consequences of history, as our students are experiencing this when they leave our classrooms. Our stories matter.

Saidya Hartman's pivotal piece, "Venus in Two Acts," reminds us of the violence of the archives, especially for bodies that only exist in the historical imaginary as a means to reinforce and sustain the very systems that render them invisible: "But I want to say more than this. I want to do more than recount the violence that deposited these traces in the archive. I want to tell a story about two girls capable of retrieving what remains dormant—the purchase or claim of their lives on the present—without committing further violence in my own act of narration."[2] As Saidya Hartman teaches us, I, too, want to listen to what is unsaid, translating misconstrued words, mindfully piecing together lives through the silences to not recreate violence. History already dispossesses communities, and our classrooms reinforce that dispossession when we silence our students and their communities' histories. But what would our classrooms and society look like if we teach to center their voices, histories, and lived experiences as not only valuable teaching lessons but tools to transform schooling experiences? Bringing in multiple voices and material possessions from our communities is vital in that work, allowing our students and communities to be both heard and seen. Our stories matter.

The dispossession faced by racialized, minoritized communities within the United States is experienced in multiple ways and spaces. What history teaches us within a K–12 context is limited in terms of the dispossession experienced by Black, Brown, and Indigenous communities, and their voices are often absent from historical text. Their experiences are read through larger historical conversations on US interventions and expansion, footnotes in the very historical processes that frame their status. How do we move these communities and, by extension, bodies from the footnotes of history and reimagine our curricular and pedagogical practices as interventions that offer our students and communities hope? How do we create and reimagine classrooms where our students see themselves as history makers, becoming teachers themselves, filling in the gaps left by curriculum standards, holes that weaponize memory by forcing us to remember a past not of our own making? Our stories matter.

Our students are the children, grandchildren, and descendants of people who have lived through the very histories we teach. As Yoon K. Pak demonstrates in her foundational text on Japanese American children in US incarceration camps during World War II, the signing of President Roosevelt's Executive Order 9066 did more than label Japanese Americans as enemies but included young students who were forced to articulate their identity amidst political turmoil. As one student wrote in 1942 as they were forcibly relocated along with thousands of other American citizens of Japanese descent, "I am sorry we have to leave. . . . Where ever I am going I wish I have a teacher like you. . . . In so many month[s] I wish the war will be over."[3] These young students perhaps did not fully understand the severity of their situation in the political moment they were forced to live in, or perhaps they understood it better than anyone else. For them, they were children who missed their schools, their friends, teachers, but most of all, home. Their dispossession is not merely a footnote in history but a reality felt through the pages of these letters. Reading firsthand letters and oral histories centers the importance of primary sources to really humanize history and, with it, teach students that these are more than just events documented in a text but lives that mattered. These letters document more than their dispossession but offer us an opportunity to position children's voices and experiences as radical tools that aid our understanding of the effects of history on the lives of those at the receiving end of policies. Primary sources such as these tell us more about how a nation viewed racialized communities as casualties of political movements and war, at times rendering bodies not only invisible but disposable. Classrooms should be spaces that honor these community histories as not just authentic in the *telling* of history but the authority in the *teaching* of history. Our stories matter.

How we teach history is not just important but critical if we hope to shift the narratives of our collective future. To be sure, the disposed have been active in articulating their lived experiences amidst the evolving social and political moments in which they live. The lesson for us is to listen to those voices, allowing them to guide our understanding of not just history but to reimagine a future that sees our communities as part of it. Centering the voices, artifacts, and memories of communities pushed to the margins is critical if we are committed to justice-oriented pedagogical practices within our schools. It is more than just teaching students how social and political movements and communities evolved and sometimes dissolved; it is about contextualizing the ways in which these communities and groups both imagined their own history, thus reshaping how others remember them. The work we do as educators and future educators is imperative. Working with students and their communities allows us to force history to recontextualize the lived and learned realities of populations and, more so, how these individuals view themselves within a larger political, economic, or social history. Our students' knowledge traditions, the collective memories that have guided their movements and experiences, offer much to learn from. Not only do individuals construct their own narratives from memories and experiences, but these narratives inform how they view the past and their positions in it. When they walk into classrooms, that past is erased or pushed to the margins of history. What message do we transmit to students when erasure is normalized, delegitimizing life experiences as antidotes? Family and community stories, ordinary lives, silenced. What these stories can do or, more importantly, what our work as researchers and educators should do, is challenge what are deemed as valuable and legitimate resources in our classrooms and in the writing of history. Reminding us that even in the most ordinary of lives, there is much to be learned from. Our stories matter.

It is a responsibility I carry with me as I enter classrooms, guiding students and future educators on our shared work, challenging them to see themselves within history—for some, for the first time. We locate one another across texts and maps, through policies informing our family and community migrations, global phenomena and military actions that would bring some of us face to face in schools and communities, the violence that separated many from their lands, and sometimes the joy of our community contributions. One by one, we begin to see one another in places we were never meant to be seen. I share with them my regret in not collecting my own family elders' oral histories before their deaths and how the film *Coco* saddens me because of it. What happens, I ask them, if there is no one left to remember us, especially when history has never made room for us? This is our challenge. I reiterate to students that we come from communities with histories, stories to tell. I teach them to engage with oral histories to help us be remembered as we find one another across history, in the hopes that they will teach others, our lives serving as lessons. But it is important to remember that the collecting of oral histories is not just something that should occur within or to benefit academic spaces, although that is important in itself. This work should be done alongside communities, especially those from which our students come, allowing the community to serve as co-teachers, and allowing our students to leave our schools with their humanity intact. Allowing communities to remind the larger society of the many contributions these lives have made in developing ideas, spaces, or, at times, witnesses to history's violent atrocities. This work, even if difficult, allows us to deconstruct or dismantle power relationships that have negated a sense of justice and belonging for so many, perpetuating the harmful effects of history. Our stories matter.

What could community and family stories, lessons, and oral histories teach us about ourselves, our communities, and societies constantly in flux as we negotiate our place in history? Family homes and kitchen tables are, at times, our students' first classrooms. Family stories offer expert accounts of histories of labor and immigration policies that have informed our lives. This work can serve larger purposes. In retelling his own family history of migration and its influence on his work as a researcher, Gabriel Rodriguez records and retells his parents' story alongside a larger telling of US Latina/o history.[4] As he reflects, his parents were his first teachers, a lesson understood as he worked to record their oral histories, helping him to truly understand the consequence of US history on his community. As historians of education have noted, for communities living, working, or fighting at the margins, oral histories can serve as placeholders for the past and work to capture the present, offering invaluable lessons about how we must position communities as experts in the telling of histories.[5] Oral histories are living embodiments of histories, sometimes erased, or histories people wish to forget to avoid holding present societies accountable for the consequences of the past. As recent debates are demonstrating, a move to "sanitize" the teaching of history across the country is growing, as is evident in places like Oklahoma and Florida. On the eve of the 100th-year commemoration of the Tulsa Race Massacre in 2021, the Oklahoma state legislature and Governor Kevin Stitt signed House Bill 1775 into law.[6] House Bill 1775's passing essentially prohibited the inclusion of curriculum or teaching that "an individual, by virtue of his or her race or sex, bears responsibility for actions committed in the past by other members of the same race or sex." Aside from not wanting to claim "responsibility" for a state's past, the bill sought to ignore Oklahoma's rich history of community activism and the contributions of communities of color. Students would be forced to learn about the history of Black, Indigenous, and other communities as merely moments, devoid of any conversation on the experiences and consequences of state-sanctioned violence across the country. How do you teach about the Tulsa

Race Massacre without engaging in a thoughtful yet difficult conversation on the history of enslavement, settler colonialism, and embodied white supremacy that allows for such atrocities to occur? Where are the voices of those most affected? How do we move away from teaching history as just moments, occurrences that frame our understanding or relationship with spaces, and instead bring in oral histories, community and family stories, as methodological interventions in our classrooms as tools to dismantle the processes that render communities invisible and silenced? Our stories matter.

Stories, especially for communities of color in the United States, are the center of life. As Angie Morill and Eve Tuck challenge us, "I think I want to know about the larger question of how do you grapple with representing vanishing without reproducing the violence of vanishing"[7] in our work as educators? However, because the teaching and learning of history are dependent on narratives captured by privileged and dominant voices and supported by archives collected by those engaged in or benefiting from our dispossession, classrooms have served to perpetuate the violence of vanishing. Perhaps the first lesson is to open our doors, extending our classrooms into our communities, dismantling notions that the only teaching that occurs is within those walls, instead viewing the community as a living archive. Teaching our students that the family stories shared along with meals serve as lessons. At least once a semester in my Latina/o history courses, one student smiles as they realize their abuelito, the person who held their hand to walk them to school every morning, was a history maker, part of the history of US labor policies via the Bracero Program. In their grandmother's boxes, hidden away for years, they come to see their family intertwined with US history, not a footnote anymore, but a lesson. A lesson I wish came earlier in their educational history. One that would have allowed them to record their abuelito's story. I sit with that as I think of how we can move to privilege the voices and histories of the very communities present within our schools, allowing them to represent their own histories as not just passive participants and victims but similarly work to center critical hope as a lens in which to translate history and events. Oral and community histories offer the opportunity to not only claim our place in history, especially for those of us oftentimes marginalized in the telling of history, but further offer the opportunity to gain a better sense of self.[8] As Yi-Fu Tuan reminds us, to strengthen our sense of self, the past needs to be rescued and made accessible."[9] Rescuing the past, especially working alongside local communities, "allows us a glimpse of historical accounts that may not be represented in the writing of history, or in the archives, because of the social hierarchy that has traditionally marked historical narratives as valid accounts of a seemingly monolithic past."[10] The past is far from homogeneous, so why should the teaching of history continue to assume that it is? How do we move my student's abuelito out of a dusty box in an attic and not recreate vanishing or violence? Our stories matter.

As Richard White reminds us, "Lives are not stories. . . . We turn our lives into stories" under our own terms.[11] Educators can use community stories and oral histories as a means to extend agency to oftentimes silenced communities to create their own spaces and frame their own histories under their own terms. Lives may not be stories, but the critical nature and inclusion of these lives can help us to rewrite the stories that have been written and taught regarding our communities for many years, absent of our own voices and accounts. It is not just about teaching history but understanding that our students and, by extension, their communities have lived through it. Communities have already been doing the work to ensure their own sobrevivencia through archival projects. Neighborhoods are living archives waiting to be discovered. We see examples of this across community spaces, forcing a shift in who we see as experts in the teaching of history. For example, Chicago's Puerto Rican community has worked to bridge these relationships with their *El Archivo*, a community archive documenting Puerto Ricans in Chicago and across the Midwest.[12] Within this space, community members share their own telling of migration stories, family histories, and images that anchor them within the city's history. The community is no longer silenced. Community members become expert historians, similarly extending these lessons to K–12 teachers and students, offering to educate the very system that has historically rendered them invisible. But we need to ensure others are listening. Our stories matter.

Our students carry stories with them as they walk into their classrooms, and our teaching should reflect that. More so, our teaching should challenge us to think intently and intentionally about what it means for us as scholars, teachers, and community members to navigate conversations on reckoning and reconciliation in education, viewing our community histories as frameworks to do so. As the authors in this collection remind us, as the United States engaged in schooling practices that simultaneously harmed and erased Black, Brown, Indigenous, and other marginalized bodies, these very communities created alternative spaces that not only supported their humanity but centered their knowledge traditions and practices. Creating these spaces, both via formal and informal schooling practices, allows history to be an intricate part of the healing process. While we may not be able to remediate the atrocities of the past, we could move beyond seeing us as mere victims and, as these chapters demonstrate, disrupt the legacies of oppression in both our students' and communities' lives. As historians, we are taught to read sources and examine evidence, but what if none exist? Recovery projects, whether through archives or oral histories, as seen in this collection of essays, are imperative to our teaching but also aid in decolonizing communities and education. Our work in this process reiterates that our existence is an act of resistance, especially in the current political moment our students both learn and live in. As Tadashi Dozono challenges us in this collection, the creativity and contributions of marginalized communities, such is the case for queer folks, disrupt these master narratives and allow these recovery projects to be an ongoing process of community interaction and remembrance. Our stories matter.

I return to my second-grade classroom. I realize now with every lesson I teach in my classrooms and every scholarly piece I publish, I begin with that moment. The joy a child feels when their name is pronounced correctly. Their home not just a pin on a map, only reappearing in one line in a high school history book years later when it is time to learn about the Spanish-American War. Home was around me, in the stories we shared, the food we learned about, the songs we sang. I tell my students home is in everything I teach and write about, unapologetically. As Gloria Anzaldúa taught us, "I am a turtle. Wherever I go I carry home on my back."[13] I carry home with me, and with it the lessons taught to me by my ancestors, my community, and with that comes the responsibility of reinserting us where history sought to erase us. Our stories matter. Now, tell me about home?

Mirelsie Velázquez, PhD

Associate Professor of Latina/o Studies

University of Illinois at Urbana-Champaign

Introduction

MARIBEL SANTIAGO AND TADASHI DOZONO

The idea for this book came from years of conversations regarding our research and experiences with history education. We have written elsewhere about the history education field's inability or unwillingness to discuss race and ethnicity. What began as a research journey stemming from our frustration led to other research on the possibilities of history education. We realized that historical inquiry is not supposed to be the endpoint. Learning to apply historical thinking skills is not the goal but instead part of a process to better understand the past. It sparked in us some hope for a field of history education that includes race and ethnicity *while* honoring and respecting those communities as agents of their past and future instead of mere history subjects. While all of this academic tension was happening, the US was in distress.

We began planning this book in 2020, during a time when whole cities were burning, protesting against the modern-day lynching of Black people. There was momentum growing from peoples' rage fueled by learning about institutionalized racism, police brutality, and how anti-Blackness permeates all aspects of our lives. We could no longer deny that discussing race and ethnicity in our classrooms and research was necessary and urgent. Those who were unfamiliar with anti-Blackness were suddenly shocked and open to learning. That moment did not last. As this project has come to fruition, renewed backlash and attacks on our bodies and ways of being have grown: anti-Asian violence and xenophobia stemming from the COVID-19 pandemic, book banning, and anti-critical race theory (CRT) legislation, alongside multiple anti-trans bills targeting youth in particular, and continued attack on immigrants and refugees.

We continued to write and edit this book during times of conflict, trying to do this work with care for each other in mind. This xenophobia and racist violence impacts us as members of these communities and as scholars who must learn to make our research palpable for an audience that oftentimes does not care or does not understand this pain. In all honesty, we are exhausted from all the hate and from having to write from a reactionary place. We are constantly, as educators and scholars, thinking about how to reframe our work for fear of how it will be perceived through a white gaze. We often muzzled ourselves for the sake of making others (mostly white scholars and educators) feel comfortable enough to read our message. We have to think strategically about how to research, write, and teach about race and ethnicity in a way that would be acceptable for a white audience who might be more concerned about historical inquiry and thinking skills and less about what students and their communities bring to the classroom. In many ways, this book is our own process of working through and healing our relationships with the history education field. Many of the chapters address healing from history-related trauma. The trauma of how our histories have been taught in schools, how we have been dismissed as agents of history, and the trauma of having to carry this work forward while being ignored. But what if, instead, we wrote from a place of possibility?

This book brings together a diverse group of authors from various racial and ethnic backgrounds, fields, and areas of research expertise to nuance historical knowledge and inquiry. The authors purposefully complicate racial and ethnic categories and their relationships to gender and queerness to challenge assumptions of homogeneity about Black, Indigenous, Latinx, Arab, and Asian American communities while highlighting and honoring their unique forms of knowledge. For example, contributors offer intersectional analyses that examine Queer of Color methods, Blackness and Indigeneity within Latinidad, immigration alongside settler colonialism, and gender with anti-Palestinian racism. This collective of scholars are experts in history education, history of education, and American studies from both Canada and the United States. Finally, as teacher educators and former K–12 teachers, these scholars connect theory to practice for classroom educators.

THE LIMITS OF A EUROCENTRIC APPROACH TO HISTORY EDUCATION

The last several decades have witnessed a shift in K–12 history pedagogy away from rote memorization of facts toward an emphasis on historical inquiry and thinking skills derived from academic historians.[1] Although scholars highlight different skills, they generally emphasize teaching students to think critically about the past and the sources they read. Thinking critically furthers historical inquiry's appeal because it reinforces students' literacy development.

Historical thinking is a welcome change to the rote memorization of facts; however, it poses two problems: prioritizing Eurocentric approaches to history and framing history as an individual cognitive act. Historical thinking stems from how historians analyze the past. But the discipline of history is rooted in European forms of scholarship[2] that have subjugated other forms of historical knowledge, including oral histories as well as non-English or non-European terminology.[3] Thus, historical thinking is the tool by which European approaches to history are manifested in K–12 classrooms. This approach is increasingly becoming more concerned with assessing whether students are acquiring a specific set of skills.[4] In reducing history to the mastery of skills, history is framed more as an individual cognitive act.

Educators committed to social justice have used historical thinking skills to emphasize historically marginalized perspectives and encourage students to consider social inequities and power dynamics.[5] Although this approach is more attuned to the interests and perspectives of Black, Indigenous, Latinx, Pacific Islander, Middle Eastern, and Asian American students, in maintaining a Eurocentric approach to historical inquiry, it inadvertently reaffirms the European mode of inquiry as *the* way to engage in historical analysis. In doing so, racial and ethnic community approaches to history can continue to be inadvertently omitted. This continues to uphold a paradigm in which Black, Indigenous, Latinx, Pacific Islander, Middle Eastern, and Asian forms of knowledge are framed as unacademic or premodern forms of engaging the past.

Our relationships with history and our methods for engaging history have been marginalized. The histories of our communities have been allowed to exist through European epistemologies to make sense of our communities, in the process cutting off communities' relationships to their own approaches to history. To be fair, historical thinking was never meant to encompass the whole person or their communities. After all, it *is* called historical *thinking*. But an emphasis on "disciplinary" knowledge and methods can dismember the racialized identity from the scholarship of Black, Indigenous, Latinx, Pacific Islander, Middle Eastern, and Asian people. The result is a form of "bifurcated thinking" that privileges Western knowledge.[6] This also results in an isolated individual cognitive process, decontextualized from communities for whom that history means something.

PARADIGM SHIFT: RACIAL AND ETHNIC COMMUNITY APPROACHES TO HISTORY ARE LEGITIMATE

Shifting the Lens in History Education's main purpose is to change how educators think about history education. We assert that racial and ethnic community approaches to history are legitimate. By racial and ethnic community approaches, we mean how those communities conceptualize history. Such approaches include a connection to land, water, and spirituality, to name a few. In today's terms, these approaches might be called "interdisciplinary," not history as its own disciplinary form of thinking. Yet, as we will describe below, racial and ethnic community approaches to history are much more than that. We respect these approaches for what they are: distinct forms of knowledge that contribute something to history education that history, the discipline, cannot.

We have identified four distinctions between traditional, inquiry-driven history education and racial and ethnic community approaches to history (although there are probably more than four). First, some of these approaches to history do not owe their origin to the history field. The authors challenge this in a couple of ways. For example, Meredith L. McCoy (Turtle Mountain Ojibwe descent) pushes against Eurocentric notions of when peoples enter history—when Europeans acknowledged and made sense of non-European peoples. Other authors highlight how racial and ethnic community approaches to history are rooted in anticolonial practices meant to challenge dominant narratives. For example, Jocyl Sacramento and Lauren Arzaga Daus recognize the failure of history textbooks to present Filipina/x/o history with agency, depth, or complexity, narrowly framed as the "Little Brown Brothers" of the United States. Instead, Sacramento and Arzaga Daus ground historical inquiry within Filipina/x/o communities through community-based practices of knowledge exchange. Eliana Castro and Krista L.

Cortes focus on a different anticolonial practice, specifically AfroIndigenous spiritual practices as a way to highlight Afrodiasporic histories. These three chapters (3, 4, and 5) demonstrate that racial and ethnic community approaches to history do not have to fit under the confines of European historical approaches. This is not to say that Eurocentric approaches to history education are not useful or that they are in contradiction with racial and ethnic community ones. Simply, historical inquiry is not the starting point of how racial and ethnic communities understand history, nor should it be the ending point.

Second, racial and ethnic approaches to history encompass more than historical thinking. The book contributors point out that the racial and ethnic community approaches to history center people and their humanity. They ask readers to push toward another direction, recentering and honoring racial and ethnic community approaches to history that can do more than historical thinking can do: they can heal. Brittany Jones, Dawnavyn James, LaGarrett J. King, and Daphanie Bibbs ask readers to consider the full spectrum of Black emotionality through their history textbook analysis and offer Jones' Critical Analysis of Racialized Emotions (CARE) as a means to address how racialized emotions interplay with historical narratives. Muna Saleh and M. Yianella Blanco each focus on a distinct form of storytelling as a means for collective healing. Saleh discusses how intergenerational Palestinian (her)storytelling challenging the erasure of Palestinian people can be a healing practice. Similarly, Blanco considers how *testimonios* in challenging dominant narratives make space for creating new ones that focus on Central American youths' joy, strengths, and wealth. Lastly, Castro and Cortes conceptualize *remediando* as a means to connect different forms of knowledge into a holistic approach that helps heal historical wounds. Centering emotions in history, rather than siloing them from analysis, is a form of resistance. It asks history education to make space for students' emotions while also challenging what is considered valid forms of historical knowledge and analysis.

Third, the contributors break out of the disciplinary confines of how communities have been made historical, of how our communities have been subjected to the disciplinary norms of history. This extends the broader reframing of racially marginalized communities from subjects to agents of history. The contributors assert models for how racially and ethnically marginalized communities can be empowered through our own capacities to be historical. McCoy directly challenges how history education, in upholding a settler narrative, has promoted a history of Indigenous erasure. She asks readers to *expect* Indigenous presence in the past and present and, therefore, make room for Indigenous peoples in the future as active agents of their own history. Jones et al. take a slightly different approach in their analysis of Black history textbooks, revealing how Black historical actors are not allowed to express rage, robbing Black people of the full range of emotion and of their full humanity. Jones et al.'s CARE framework offers educators a tool to support students in engaging in critical analysis of how Black emotionality is addressed through historical narratives. Tadashi Dozono offers examples of how queer Scholars of Color have intervened in dominant practices within the history discipline, offering methods for reading the archive in the face of historical silencing and negation.

Fourth, whereas history education emphasizes *doing* history (inquiry and thinking), racial and ethnic community approaches to history focus on what history *does*. This book aims to shift from a focus on isolated skills to process: history *does* something with community. For example, testimonios and storytelling are more than reading a primary source. Storytelling is a socially contextualized act happening with and within the community. This interaction leaves an impact on those who participate and the community. One of the main changes that the book contributors describe is the process of healing. This impact on the individual and community, or what history *does*, expands the notion of history. Blanco, Saleh, and Sacramento and Arzaga Daus all focus on forms of storytelling that are both specific to their communities and also have to be done *with* community. Testimonios, Palestinian (her)storytelling, and Kuwentuhan cannot be done individually in isolation. They are meant as a means of learning in community.

Rather than value the conventional historical thinking approach as the center, this volume centers ways of knowing and thinking about history from racially marginalized spaces, inclusive of Black, Indigenous, Latinx, Middle Eastern, and Asian knowledge formations. *Shifting the Lens in History Education* brings the question of what the future of history education should look like back to the communities that have been historically marginalized.

HOW THIS BOOK IS ORGANIZED: CONTEXT AND FRAMEWORK, THINKING HOLISTICALLY, AND STORYTELLING AS HEALING

Shifting the Lens in History Education is organized into three parts. The first part, "Context and Framework" (chapters 1 and 2), sets the historical and theoretical foundation for the book. The coeditors each offer a chapter that situates the works of the contributing authors. The second part, "Thinking Holistically" (chapters 3 through 5), asks students and teachers to consider humans in the present and the past with all their emotional complexity. The last part, "Storytelling as Healing" (chapters 6 through 8), offers three different examples of storytelling as a form of historical inquiry *and* healing. Collectively, these three parts encourage the reader to reconsider how racial and ethnic community approaches to history are expansive, legitimate, community-oriented, and healing.

PART ONE: CONTEXT AND FRAMEWORK

In this part, Maribel Santiago and Tadashi Dozono set the historical and theoretical tone of the book. In chapter 1, "The Legacy of Racial and Ethnic Community-Led Education," Santiago delves into the broader historical context behind racial and ethnic community approaches to history that the contributing authors discuss. These approaches are part of intergenerational movements that challenge white hegemonic historical approaches. After providing a brief overview of the purpose of schooling, Santiago gives examples of how Black, Indigenous, Mexican, and Asian-origin communities created their own educational spaces to resist US public schooling. The chapter concludes with common themes from these educational spaces and connects the work of the contributing authors to the over 150-year legacy of racial and ethnic community-led education.

Chapter 2, "Queer of Color Horizons: Reorienting History Education Through Queer of Color Methods," offers examples of queer Scholars of Color whose work pushes the history discipline to account for doing history from a position of marginalization. Tadashi Dozono argues incorporating students' queer and racialized identities into historical inquiry allows teachers to highlight the tensions between identity and difference and orientation and disorientation. Dozono makes explicit how including students' own identities in historical analysis can shape their understanding of who they are, as well as important differences in how people understood themselves in the past. By forefronting how queer Scholars of Color engage problems within the history discipline, Dozono sets the disciplinary stage for why the subsequent chapters are needed.

PART TWO: THINKING HOLISTICALLY

Part two offers three examples of how the teaching of history can and should include a more holistic representation of historical subjects, specifically Indigenous,

Black, and AfroIndigenous peoples. Chapter 3, "Expecting Indigenous Presence: Indigenous Pasts, Presents, and Futures in K–12 Social Studies," presents an argument for a new way of teaching about Native histories that engages with Indigenous life in a more complex and holistic way. To engage more fully with Indigenous histories, presents, and futures, Meredith McCoy supports readers in developing a habit of *expecting Indigenous presence.* "Presence" refers to the holistic, complicated, large- and small-scale, everyday stories of Indigenous people, both in response to and entirely separate from histories of colonial violence. In helping students learn to expect Indigenous life, they will become adults who are ready to hear messy, complex, and whole stories of Indigenous people, past, present, and future. McCoy provides an array of already available Indigenous-created resources, including oral histories, blogs, and children's books, to center Indigenous voices and experiences in your classrooms to guide educators of all backgrounds in this work.

Chapter 4, "We Have Joy but What About Rage? An Examination of Race and Emotions," offers another take on what happens when we do not consider people with their full humanity. Specifically, Brittany Jones, Dawnavyn James, LaGarrett J. King, and Daphanie Bibbs argue that even well-intentioned books that focus on Blackness do not always make space for Black emotions, or at least the ones that are not considered acceptable. Based on findings from a study that examined how the Black History 365 fourth- and fifth-grade textbooks depicted Black people's emotions, the authors found that the textbooks focused exclusively on Black people's joy. The books make no explicit reference to the rage or anger that Black people felt in the past. The authors argue that textbooks and other curricular materials dehumanize and erase Black agency from Black historical narratives when they solely focus on Black joy. Additionally, the authors assert that teaching through the full range of Black emotionality can strengthen the teaching of Black histories. The chapter concludes by introducing readers to CARE, a framework that guides students through a critical analysis of racialized emotions. The authors posit that CARE can be a useful framework when teaching Black emotions during Black history instruction and that CARE can also strengthen students' historical thinking skills and their historical empathy.

Finally, Eliana Castro and Krista L. Cortes's chapter connects the argument for holistic approaches to healing, the theme of part three. Chapter 5, "'Remediando' Latinx Blackness: AfroIndigenous Spiritual Practice as History Pedagogy," offers AfroIndigenous spiritual practices as a type and means of knowledge formation. They propose a form of teaching for reclamation and resistance that (re)centers students' racialized experiences and serves as a healing practice. Castro and Cortes draw parallels between AfroIndigenous spiritual practices of their ancestors and the application of those principles in history education. This approach constitutes what they call remediando, or healing—a model of teaching and learning that emulates key features of AfroIndigenous spiritual practices. They conclude with examples of how these strategies may look in a K–12 classroom and offer resources for educators.

PART THREE: STORYTELLING AS HEALING

In each of the three chapters in part three, the authors offer distinct yet overlapping examples of how storytelling has been and continues to be an important community practice for inquiring into the past. The authors push back against the history discipline's dismissal of storytelling to reveal the community and cultural importance of storytelling as an act done in practice within community.

In chapter 6, "Embracing Palestinian Oral Histories and Narratives in History Education," Muna Saleh explores how embracing intergenerational Palestinian (her)storytelling holds educative potential for history education. Interweaving the author's autobiographical narratives with the literature, Saleh narratively explores what they imagine as a *pedagogy of Palestinian (her)storytelling.* This chapter argues that centering the experiences of Palestinian students, educators, and families/caregivers can provide life-affirming counterstories to dominant (Eurocentric, colonial, racist, and misogynist) narratives in history education. After reading this chapter, educators will better understand, center, and uplift the importance of oral traditions and storytelling to/in (liberatory) history education—in particular, the intergenerational knowledges and wisdoms of Palestinian (her) storytelling.

In chapter 7, "Centering Pinxy Narratives: Kuwentos and Kuwentuhan in History Education," Jocyl Sacramento and Lauren Arzaga Daus center Filipina/x/o American kuwentos and kuwentuhan as a method of inquiry within history education. Filipina/x/o kuwentos, or stories, bring forth perspectives that have been marginalized or omitted from white, colonial narratives often taught within history classrooms. Kuwentos act as a form of resistance to universal ways of learning.

Engaging kuwentos and practicing kuwentuhan, or the process of storytelling, disrupts linear models of historical inquiry and recognizes students as active agents in history-making. Kuwentuhan can be a strategy for knowledge exchange in the classroom and can also be used as a method of inquiry when collecting and analyzing data for research. Kuwentuhan allows students and teachers to engage in relational interaction to place their own and their families' experiences within a larger socio-historical-political context when learning history.

Chapter 8, "Testimonio as Healing Praxis in History Classrooms," explores the healing possibilities of testimonio in history classrooms. M. Yianella Blanco introduces the potential of testimonio as a pedagogical and curricular tool when learning about the histories and experiences of Central America(ns), little of which is currently taught in schools despite the growing population of Central Americans in the United States. Testimonio, a genre within Latin American and Indigenous oral traditions, has been used by individuals to challenge dominant narratives by "situating the individual in communion with a collective experience marked by marginalization, oppression, or resistance."[7] The results from this chapter demonstrate that testimonios can aid in dismantling oppressive narratives *and* building new ones focused on Latinx youths' joy, strengths, and wealth. The teachers in the study offer practical examples of how they would teach more nuanced histories of migration.

HOW TO USE THIS BOOK

Shifting the Lens in History Education is intended for both educators and education researchers. The scholars in this volume apply different lenses for addressing histories that are often ignored in the classroom. We reconceptualize what are considered legitimate forms of historical knowledge and encourage educators to include them alongside disciplinary approaches. Each chapter centers approaches to historical inquiry arising from racially and ethnically minoritized communities within history classrooms. This volume complicates how race and ethnicity are addressed in history pedagogy, from mere content knowledge to forms of analysis and inquiry that extend conventional approaches to history. This paradigm shift is necessary for history teachers to center their racially and ethnically marginalized students' historical approaches.

Throughout each chapter, teacher educators, history teachers, and history education researchers will learn to shift how disciplinary expertise and knowledge are defined in the teaching of history. This book does not mean to replace, but to be in conversation with conventional resources for disciplinary learning to honor the knowledge of students' communities as legitimate forms of knowledge alongside the dominant paradigm of historical inquiry rooted in European methods.

Shifting the Lens in History Education is for educators who want to extend their classrooms beyond conventional approaches to historical inquiry to center approaches to history arising from students' racial and ethnic communities. This book encourages current teachers to shift the focus of their curriculum beyond state standards and narrowly defined historical disciplinary skills and consider approaches to history that align more closely with their racially and ethnically marginalized students' racialized experiences and knowledge. We also challenge education researchers to shift how they define the history discipline, the methods of inquiry, and epistemic lineages that inform historical inquiry in the classroom.

This book, however, is not a "how-to" book. We ask readers to critically reflect on their own positionality and caution against cultural appropriation. For example, rather than have students reenact a cultural practice, students might engage a source by someone from that cultural community modeling a particular practice and consider how their community engages in historical inquiry.

PART ONE

Context and Framework

CHAPTER 1

The Legacy of Racial and Ethnic Community-Led Education

MARIBEL SANTIAGO

For as long as public schools have existed in the United States, racial and ethnic communities have challenged how schools privilege dominant European forms of knowledge—specifically those rooted in Protestant values. While US public schools prioritized subordination and assimilationist policies, racial and ethnic communities created alternate educational spaces where they emphasized community knowledge. Not all racial and ethnic communities resisted in the same way, nor did they all have the same priorities. Their approaches were responsive to their distinct needs. But what is consistent across the Black, Indigenous, Mexican, and Asian-origin communities in this chapter is a determination to create spaces that honor students' racial and ethnic cultural backgrounds and heal them from the Americanization and dehumanized processes that they encountered in schools.

This chapter provides readers with a historical background for the racial and ethnic community approaches to history that the other contributing authors discuss. The purpose is to contextualize these racial and ethnic community approaches to history as part of the legacy of an intergenerational movement that challenged white hegemonic historical approaches. To understand why racial and ethnic communities resisted US public schooling, this chapter first offers a brief overview of the purpose of schooling. The second section offers examples of how

Black, Indigenous, Mexican-origin, and Asian-origin communities created their own educational spaces to emphasize cultural knowledge and practices in response to schooling systems. The third section focuses on the common themes across these educational spaces, specifically that they functioned as forms of resistance and the major role that retaining home language played in this effort. In the conclusion, I connect the work of the contributing authors to the over 150-year legacy of racial and ethnic community approaches to history.

This is by no means an exhaustive history of racial and ethnic community-led educational spaces in the US. This chapter offers a few examples that contextualize the subsequent chapters' specific movements and knowledge formations within a broader history of schooling. For example, I try to focus more on racial and ethnic community-led educational spaces prior to the 1950s, as this history is lesser known in our historical consciousness than the efforts related to the civil rights and power movements. I also do not focus on school segregation or boarding schools as this was not a response to public schooling but rather how public schooling was enacted against Black, Indigenous, Mexican, and Asian-origin communities. I also acknowledge that I am sharing histories documented in books and articles, many of which focus on the western US. There are many other examples of racial and ethnic community-led educational spaces that resisted Americanization and dehumanization efforts that have not been shared beyond their communities. As such, this chapter focuses on Black, Indigenous, Mexican, Chinese, and Japanese-origin communities for which there exists documentation.

COMPULSORY SCHOOLING, COMPULSORY ASSIMILATION

Since their inception, US schools have privileged European forms of knowledge. Founders of the US—influenced by the European Enlightenment—believed that leaders of the country should be highly educated.[1] Some, including Thomas Jefferson, supported public elementary schooling for "all of the free children, male and female."[2] Although neither compulsory nor accessible to all, a public school system was proposed as early as 1778.[3] However, it was not until 1852 that Massachusetts became the first state to make schooling mandatory for children.[4]

The push for a public school system stemmed from the belief that an educated citizenry was essential for the well-being of the nation. Proponents of the common school movement advocated for "universal" access to schools to promote morality, democracy, and literacy.[5] As mandatory schooling was expanded, larger, bureaucratic schooling systems replaced small, community-run schools.[6] The perceived efficiency and impartiality of the hierarchies observed in factories and businesses influenced this new system.[7] As schools expanded, so did their assimilationist practices. Reformers believed there were singular best practices that would work to teach increasingly diverse students in every school. This would eventually lead to the establishment of compulsory school attendance national legislation in 1918.[8]

What was considered beneficial for the nation, however, was not necessarily in line with racial and ethnic community approaches to education. More immigrant children and children of immigrants attended schools as the compulsory school movement gained traction. The slowly changing demographics led to an increase in assimilation policies in schools. But, of course, these were grounded in European Protestant values. Many Irish and Italian-origin children, despite being racially white, were considered inferior because of their Catholic beliefs and in need of Americanization.[9] As such, it was specifically European Protestant values that framed the schooling system in the US.

Forced to educate Black, Indigenous, Latinx, and Asian American children, even if in segregated public schools, officials continued their dehumanization and assimilationist practices. Despite calls for unification, Black, Indigenous, and Mexican-origin students (as well as other students of color) were never thought to be part of the unification.[10] Black community members "learned that the educational system that was to homogenize other Americans was not meant for them."[11] "Intelligence" testing became part of this rhetoric, part of the larger eugenics movement to claim that Black, Indigenous, Latinx, and Asian American and immigrant students were genetically inferior and therefore should be prepared for manual labor.[12]

It is important to note that the national schooling system for Indigenous children did not function on the same timeline as that of Black, Latinx, Asian American, and Pacific Islander students. For example, the Indian Civilization Act that established Native American boarding schools was passed in 1819, almost a hundred years before compulsory education. The government's determination to eliminate Indigenous nations and to dispossess them from their land began soon after the US became a country and, in some instances, before.[13]

CREATING THEIR OWN RACIAL AND ETHNIC COMMUNITY-LED EDUCATIONAL SPACES

As public schools slowly gained traction across the nation, Black, Indigenous, Mexican, Chinese, and Japanese-origin communities established educational spaces for their children. Their parallel growth was a response to US public schools that initially excluded them and attempted to maintain their second-class status as manual labor and Americanize their children. In this sense, racial and ethnic community-led schools aimed to both provide an education where there were no schools and resist Americanization efforts. As US public schools emphasized white Protestant values and European knowledge, Black, Indigenous, Mexican, Chinese, and Japanese-origin communities feared the loss of community practices and knowledge. As such, they created educational spaces where children could maintain their cultural practices and knowledge. Each group had their own unique contexts, which provided them with varying degrees of control and agency to establish their own educational spaces. Given that each racial and ethnic community-led effort responded to their unique needs, I discuss each on their own.

Black Community-Led Educational Spaces

Before a national compulsory education system was created in 1918, there were localized efforts to create schooling opportunities. Local and state officials varied in the type of schools they established and who could access them. As such, racial and ethnic communities adapted to the distinct policies that were enacted against them.

As politicians advocated for public schooling for white children in the late 1700s, so did Black Bostonians. In 1787 and 1796, Black Bostonians petitioned the state to create a separate school for their children. The purpose was twofold: to ensure that their children could have access to an education and to shield them from discrimination in a public school system. Despite Boston school officials denying the petition, Black residents opened the African School in 1798.[14]

The African School was founded on an emerging Black nationalist ideology that taught "racial solidarity, African pride, self-sufficiency, separation, self-determination, and Black emigration."[15] This Black nationalism stemmed from "the impulse toward self-determination among Africans transplanted to the New World by the slave trade."[16] The school promoted an early version of Black nationalism and also civic participation. The schools empowered children with the intent to develop an independent and self-reliant Black community.

The African School's success was short-lived, in operation for three years only.[17] "White officials were troubled by the Black community's increasing cultural autonomy and political participation in private and public spaces." For example, Black Bostonians formed organizations, like the Anti-Colonization Committee, to counter the white supremacist organizations.[18] The African School undermined Americanization efforts in educating a community that was supposed to remain a labor force dependent on whites. The African School was a threat to white communities. "White Boston school officials later coopted the African School to legalize second-class education for Black children."[19]

Black Southerners encountered a different type of schooling challenge than in Boston. Enslaved Black children and adults were legally forbidden from learning to read or write for fear that it would encourage them to liberate themselves.[20] The Reconstruction Era, however, offered Black Southerners more educational opportunities that coincided with a growing movement toward compulsory schooling. Most white Southerners, however, resisted universal schooling, especially for Black children. Southern whites feared that educated Black citizenry would undermine their ruling power.[21]

When Black schools run by white educators did exist in the South, they were designed to keep Black southerners as a subordinate class. For example, white educators supported schools for newly freed Black students but only to teach them a "proper deference for their superiors, fidelity to contracts, respect for property, the rewards of industriousness and other virtues calculated to ensure a compliant and efficient labor force."[22] The lack of schools that academically prepared Black children prompted a need for Black-community-led schools.

Black communities created their own systems of common schooling, secondary schooling, and higher education in the South, despite white economic, social, and political forces that attempted to thwart their efforts.[23] As early as 1865, the Freedmen's Bureau reported efforts of Black individuals and communities to educate themselves, referring to them as "native schools." By 1866, there were about five hundred "native schools."[24] Segregated schools continued until *Brown v. Board of Education* in 1954. But between the Reconstruction Era and *Brown*, many Black schools thrived.[25]

The end of segregation helped initiate a second wave of educational spaces. With the mandated desegregation of the 1964 Civil Rights Act, schools were closed, and students were moved to meet desegregation requirements. Black students were often mistreated in desegregated schools and were placed in lower-level academic tracks.[26] New forms of Black-community-led educational spaces as resistance developed as a response. Community-led schools for Black children flourished in the 1960s and 1970s as a central component of the civil rights and Black Power movements. Freedom Schools emphasized a culturally relevant curriculum alongside political organizing and the usual academic subjects. Unlike the Freedom Schools, Pan-African nationalist schools were rooted in a "critique of white cultural hegemony" and emphasized Black culture and self-determination. They drew on political thinkers from the African diaspora.[27]

Black community-led educational spaces varied in their purpose and systems. Some schools targeted young children, while others were institutions of higher education. Despite existing across the country and addressing the needs of their local communities, the schools generally held two common commitments. The first was that Black community-led educational spaces emphasized preparing students to participate in active civic life for the betterment of Black people. The second is that in educating Black students, the schools rejected negative stereotypes regarding Blackness.

Mexican-Origin Community-Led Educational Spaces

The United States annexed half of Mexico's territory as the compulsory education movement gained traction. As these territories became states, they also had to consider the issue of educating Mexican-origin children. Texas had to contend with formalized Americanization efforts as early as 1854 when Texas passed the Common School Law.[28] Mexican-origin families in Illinois encountered these efforts sixteen years later, in 1870, when Illinois made compulsory education required for all students.[29] Greater access to schools came with dehumanization. In the Southwest, students were punished, sometimes physically, for speaking Spanish in schools and were often forced to Anglicize their names until the late twentieth century.[30] In Texas and California, English became the only language of instruction. In 1870, California imposed legislation that required all schools to teach in English. A year later, the Texas Superintendent of Instruction implemented policies that explicitly limited the amount of bilingualism in schools and classrooms.[31]

The lack of schools and the emphasis on Americanization in the schools that did exist prompted Mexican-origin families to create educational spaces for their children. Known as escuelitas, or little schools, they were community-initiated, funded, and controlled.[32] As community-controlled schools, they developed their own curriculum grounded in Mexican culture, identity, philosophy, and Spanish language. With no common curriculum across the various escuelitas, they were each distinct in how they developed the schools and approached the education of their Mexican-origin children.

Escuelitas existed across the nation, with Texas being one of the states with the greatest number of them. One of the longest-running escuelitas was Colegio Altamirano which was in operation from 1897 through 1958.[33] Colegio Altamirano was established in Hebbronville twenty-four years before the Hebbronville Independent School District, thus creating an educational space for Mexican-origin children where one did not exist yet. Other existing public schools in the region offered a poor quality education in humble facilities with poorly prepared teachers.[34] Colegio Altamirano stood in stark contrast. Its students were often better prepared for high school than their non-Colegio Altamirano counterparts.[35] In academically preparing children for public school, Colegio Altamirano changed the deficit narratives about Mexican-origin children.

Tejano families in Hebbronville did not see preparing their children to participate in the US and retaining Mexican identity as dichotomous. On the contrary, it was their Mexican origin that would allow them to excel. As one Colegio Altamirano alum described, "We understand our race, and when we are able to comprehend American ideas and ideals, American ways and customs, we shall be worth twice as much as they [whites]. And we certainly shall have the advantage over them."[36] In this sense, Colegio Altamirano prepared children to become "bicultural, bilingual as a means to excel. A bicultural existence was essential in the new social order."[37] Although they, too, emphasized Mexican history, culture, and knowledge, they saw biculturalism as a way to navigate the social and political demands of the US.

Meanwhile, in Chicago, Mexican-origin families were leading alternative schools as early as 1910. These schools focused on teaching children Mexican history, geography, and Spanish. Because each school was run by local community members, each school was different. However, they shared some similarities in educational purpose and ideology. Families in Chicago feared a "demexicanization" process in schools that devalued Mexican culture and knowledge and, therefore, emphasized Mexican history, culture, and philosophy.[38]

The purpose and ideology of these schools were based on a form of transnational pedagogy that was rooted in the Mexican political climate at the time—specifically the Mexican Revolution (1910–1920). Many of the Chicago area alternative schools were framed around a 1920s nationalist identity and philosophy that permeated during and after the Mexican Revolution.[39] They were heavily influenced by Mexico's "struggle for political and economic freedom, including the need for labor organizing, separation of church and state, and the need for free press and speech."[40] In this sense, escuelitas were founded on Mexican Revolutionary ideals.

Even though Colegio Altamirano was "initially funded through middle-class Tejanos and later continued with mutualista (Mexican-origin community-based mutual aid groups) support," it too had a revolutionary philosophical basis.[41] For example, the Altamirano school was named after Mexican philosopher Ignacio Manuel Altamirano shortly after his death. Altamirano was an Indigenous Mexican nationalist, novelist, and philosopher.[42] As a "poet, critic, novelist, historian, educator, diplomat, and politician, Altamirano was a liberal among liberals."[43] Altamirano was a leader in establishing Mexican national ideals.[44] Naming the school after him was reflective of the mission and values of the school.

Since US public schools often enacted English-only policies, teaching Mexican-origin children Spanish became increasingly important. One of the main ways that Mexican-origin community-led schools taught their children Spanish was through reading materials from Mexico. Hebbronville families relied on their proximity to Tamaulipas, Mexico, to access curricular resources in Spanish and hire Mexican teachers. Other escuelitas in Texas used Mexican newspapers as one of the main forms of providing reading materials to students. Educators also relied on reading materials from revolutionaries like El Partido Liberal de México.

The presence of escuelitas and other Mexican-origin community-led schools in different parts of the nation, both concurrently and decades apart, and their grounding in revolutionary ideology are more than a coincidence. They speak to how Mexican-origin communities across the nation resisted Americanization efforts that devalued their community knowledge and culture.

Asian-Origin Community-Led Educational Spaces

Although Black and Mexican-origin community-led schools are the most documented, they were not the only racial/ethnic groups to advocate for an education. Around the same time that escuelitas in Texas and Chicago were being established, Chinese- and Japanese-origin communities were establishing their own educational spaces. Chinese immigrants settled in California, whereas Japanese immigrants initially settled in Hawai'i. Despite differing circumstances in these enclaves, they shared a commitment to ensuring their children were taught their respective community's knowledge and values.

The California Gold Rush (1848–1855) and the need for additional labor to build the transcontinental railroad (1860s) were two of the major causes of Chinese immigration to the US. As Chinese immigrant laborers created families and began to set down roots in the US, they began to advocate for new needs.[45] In 1859, Chinese-origin families began to demand that their children receive public education, as they paid taxes just like other communities. In response, the San Francisco School Board opened a public school specifically for Chinese-origin students. The school, however, was poorly attended and poorly funded. Parents had no say in the instruction for their children. Furthermore, their children had to commute to a white neighborhood where white children harassed them. As a result of the poor attendance and poor funding, the school district closed the school within four months.[46]

In lieu of the poorly run school Chinese-origin parents found alternative educational spaces for their children, specifically private Chinese Heritage Language (CHL) schools. These schools were run by Chinese-origin teachers with the "explicit purpose of teaching and maintaining the traditional Chinese culture and values."[47] The first CHL school was established in San Francisco in 1886.

Chinese Heritage Language Schools exist today, primarily as weekend schools. They continue to counter Americanization schooling systems that have "been reluctant to support the maintenance of Chinese heritage language and culture for Chinese immigrant children."[48] These schools, like escuelitas, did not have a uniform curriculum because they ran largely independently of each other. For example, emphasizing Mandarin or Cantonese varies based on the mission of the founders and the needs of the community.[49] The current schools can be considered a response to a schooling system that continues to ignore Chinese history and culture. In this sense, current CHL schools continue the legacy of the work established in the late 1850s.

The other Asian-origin community whose educational spaces have also been well-documented are Japanese language schools in Hawai'i. The need for labor in the Territory of Hawai'i largely prompted Japanese arrival. Sugar plantation owners, facing a labor shortage, encouraged Japanese immigration to provide labor for the cane fields. By the 1920s, the Japanese diaspora (or Nikkei) in Hawai'i was 40 percent of the population.[50] As a result, Hawai'i became an important site for Japanese community-led schools.

Japanese-origin families, Buddhist temples, and Christian churches established the first Japanese language schools in Hawai'i. They were usually a form of supplemental education, a space where Nikkei children could hold on to their culture in response to Americanization efforts. Although they were originally created for religious purposes, Japanese language schools developed into centers that also taught Japanese culture and history. Japanese language schools functioned as the "center of issei community activities, where not only Japanese language was taught[;] . . . they represented Japanese ethnic culture, value, and pride, and were the source of ethnic identity."[51] As such, Japanese language schools relied on their homeland for resources and instruction.[52] This also ensured that the school curriculum aligned with Japanese values and knowledge.

Japanese language schools were highly successful in that they had a broad reach throughout all the islands. Within thirty years, there were over 163 Japanese language schools in Hawai'i. By the early 1920s, these schools served 98 percent of the over 20,000 Nikkei students in Hawai'i's public schools.[53] "More than 90% of school-age Nisei (second generation) concurrently attended Japanese language schools every day after public school."[54] As a result of their prominence, other Japanese communities in California and Washington used Japanese language schools in Hawai'i as a model for their own schools.[55] However, the schools on the mainland never had the same reach as those on Hawai'i.

Japanese language schools' educational approach became the excuse for them slowly being attacked. Whites in Hawai'i feared that Japanese language schools inhibited Nikkei assimilation. This fear primarily stemmed from that of white voters in Hawai'i that they would lose electoral power. Almost half of the Nikkei population in Hawai'i was Nisei, and as US-born citizens, they had a right to vote. Fearing a Nisei voting bloc, whites in Hawai'i sought to limit their power.[56] Similar to Black communities in the South, Japanese communities were seen strictly as labor. Any education that might support active civic participation was interpreted as a threat to white dominance.

Educators in Japanese language schools made compromises to try to ward off the closure of their schools. However, the forced incarceration of Nikkei in the US during World War II would eventually lead to the closure of all Japanese language schools. Some schools would eventually reopen after the end of the war. Incarcerated educators and priests who returned to Hawai'i played an important role in this effort. By May of 1949, sixty-seven schools had reopened with 11,631 students.[57] This was significantly less than the more than 163 schools and over 20,000 students that were enrolled at the height of the Japanese language school movement.

Indigenous Community-Led Educational Spaces

Schooling for Indigenous children was distinct from that for Black, Mexican-origin, and Asian-origin students. First, efforts to "educate" them predate compulsory schooling. Education was an essential tool of European settler colonialism in North America. White colonizers sought to "civilize" Indigenous people and eradicate their histories, languages, and cultures through European models of schooling.[58] Indigenous individuals, communities, and nations manipulated public schooling to resist colonial education. They created their own schooling systems and trained Indigenous educators to effectively teach their students.

Schools were considered a more effective means of controlling Indigenous peoples than military force.[59] Some Indigenous communities chose to use this push for education to their benefit. The Choctaw Nation opened Choctaw Academy, with funding from the federal government, in 1825. Choctaw leaders wanted young people—almost exclusively the male children of the tribal elites—to participate in Western schooling so they would be better equipped to assert their rights. Choctaw Academy students learned a variety of subjects, ranging from grammar to algebra to astronomy. Indigenous students connected their learnings in school with their tribal histories and knowledges to develop their own intellectual traditions and political and economic pursuits.[60] Students publicly challenged racist notions of Indigenous inferiority through publications and debates, connected their nations to global contestations of colonization, and asserted their peoples' modernity. Graduates of Choctaw Academy went on to open schools across the South and Southeast, many of which were more inclusive to all Indigenous students. Though some at the time criticized graduates for moving too far away from their indigeneity, others saw the academy as helping to prepare Indigenous men to advocate for their nations and tribes against the growing power of the US government.[61]

Throughout the twentieth century, Indigenous nations and communities took control of the Bureau of Indian Affairs and federally run schools to manage them themselves. In 1974, there were seventy-four American Indian and Alaska Native bilingual and bicultural education programs.[62] During the American Indian Movement (AIM) in the 1960s and 1970s, "survival" schools were founded by Indigenous people in cities to better serve Indigenous students. Indigenous educators taught Indigenous language, history, skills, culture, philosophy, religion, and wellness.

The Red School House in Saint Paul, Minnesota, and Heart of the Earth school in Minneapolis, Minnesota, exemplified the mission of survival schools. Opened in 1972 by AIM activists, these schools were intentionally designed to support the needs of urban Indigenous students in the Twin Cities.[63] Students were organized by age and academic ability rather than by rigid grade levels. Both schools were staffed entirely by Indigenous educators, parents, and community members who prioritized building positive relationships with students and connecting with students' lives outside of school. Students received individualized instruction and were also encouraged to work together and support the learning of other students. The academic programs promoted three goals: foster positive identity development for Indigenous youth, develop political consciousness, and center families and communities.[64]

In addition to public school subjects like math, educators also included curricula according to student interests and community needs, like drug education and graphic design. The survival schools allowed students to explore their indigeneity, build meaningful relationships with people in their families and communities, value school as a place of learning and support, and become involved in activism. The Red School House closed in 1996, and the Heart of Earth School (later renamed Oh Day Aki) closed in 2008. Yet, hundreds of young Indigenous people were nurtured by educators who resisted the harmful narratives and structures of public schooling. Survival schools also helped preserve tribal languages, histories, and knowledge that were threatened by decades of forced/coerced urbanization. By making their own schools, Indigenous communities were able to educate their children in ways that would sustain them and enable them to demand their rights.[65]

Their historical context led to Indigenous-led educational spaces that differed from that of Black, Mexican-origin, and Asian-origin communities. Settler colonialism devastated Indigenous nations and peoples in specific ways that are not comparable to the immigrant experiences of Chinese- and Japanese-origin communities. The US-Mexico War displaced Mexican-origin communities but offered them citizenship rights that were denied to Indigenous peoples until 1924.[66] Chinese-, Japanese-, and Mexican-origin communities benefitted from immigration replenishment that allowed these communities to grow. Despite attempts to eradicate Indigenous peoples and nations, they found ways to resist the specific challenges they encountered.

COMMUNITY-LED EDUCATION AS FORMS OF RESISTANCE

These racial and ethnic community-led schools are forms of educational resistance. I acknowledge that those who created, led, and attended these schools might not describe them as such. But being an alternative to a compulsory education system that dehumanized Black, Indigenous, Mexican-origin, and Asian-origin children was defiance. The racial and ethnic community-led educational spaces exemplify resistance in educating their children and ensuring that they retained their cultural practices and knowledge.

The US public education system did not initially intend to educate Black, Indigenous, Latinx, and Asian American children. Not including them in the public schooling system and then segregating them in poorly funded schools is evidence of that.[67] When forced to educate them, compulsory schools focused on Americanizing children and preparing them for manual labor. Thus, simply teaching reading, writing, and math was a form of resisting the stereotype that they were unintelligent and unteachable.

Part of the process of ensuring that Black, Indigenous, Mexican-origin, and Asian-origin communities stayed submissive and ensuring white dominance required that their children be stripped of their cultural knowledge. Thus, creating systems that allowed these communities to pass their knowledge to other generations directly challenged white supremacist structures in the US. Consider how instituting English-only policies denied Indigenous, Mexican-origin, and Asian-origin communities cultural connections and part of their humanity. This is, in large part, why language replenishment was a vital concern in Mexican-, Chinese-, and Japanese-origin communities. This is also why Indigenous-led schools also emphasized language revitalization efforts. Language is one of the major conduits for preserving community practices and knowledge. Although English was the necessary language, Spanish, Mandarin, Japanese, and differing Indigenous languages were the languages of defiance. Retaining one's home language was not only challenged negative stereotypes of Mexican, Chinese, Japanese-origin, and Indigenous communities and bilingualism, but it was also considered the main mechanism for retaining their community identity, culture, and ideals. Given that US public schools emphasized European forms of knowledge, enacted English-only policies and other assimilationist practices, racial and ethnic community-led educational spaces were pivotal to helping them preserve their cultural practices and knowledge.

CONCLUSION: WHY CENTER RACIAL AND ETHNIC COMMUNITY KNOWLEDGE

With this brief overview of over 150 years of racial and ethnic community-led educational spaces, I hope to contextualize for the reader that what the contributing authors of this volume are describing is not new. Their work is part of a legacy of educational resistance that has fought against the dehumanization and subordination of Black, Indigenous, Mexican-origin, and Asian-origin children. The contributing authors center racial and ethnic community knowledge to honor students' racial and ethnic cultural backgrounds and heal them from the Americanization and dehumanized processes that they encountered in schools. This is an extension of the curriculum that racial and ethnic community-led schools offered but within US public school settings.

Part of this tradition of resisting white hegemony in educational spaces is the ability to teach freely beyond the boundaries of the white gaze. Compulsory education always had white students in mind—the curriculum assumed a white student and, therefore, the need for the curriculum to be relevant to them. The

Black, Indigenous, Mexican-origin, and Asian-origin educational spaces described in this chapter always assumed, and therefore centered, their children as participants in the curriculum they developed. Free of the white gaze, they could center the needs of their children. The authors continue in that tradition, knowing that the pedagogical practices they are describing now must exist inside public schools. Despite this, the authors strive to move from a reactionary curriculum to an aspirational one where Black, Indigenous, Latinx, and Asian-origin children can exist in public schools along with their racial and ethnic community approaches to knowledge.

CHAPTER 2

Queer of Color Horizons: Reorienting History Education Through Queer of Color Methods

TADASHI DOZONO

In ninth grade, I took an area studies class on European history. The semester culminated in a research paper about any topic related to the class. I chose to study the *Entartete Kunst* exhibits by Nazi Germany, organized to lambaste so-called degenerate art, including German expressionism, for being grotesque and distorted in contrast to the Nazi's promotion of idealized beauty and perfected nature. I did not realize it then, but this was my attempt to engage the queer within history. I now understand that my interest in the degenerate art exhibits was my way of engaging the past queerly. My only exposure to queerness in school was having been taught by a teacher how to play "smear the queer" in elementary school, and learning from my peers that being gay was something people made fun of. When you have been taught that you are bad, but you know you are not, you seek out other examples that speak to that experience.

As a burgeoning queer youth, I was not seeking an exact replica of myself in the past but instead sought others who experienced alienation, who were cast out, deemed to have something wrong with them, and shamed for expressing their difference. Would I have benefited from teachers including content about queer Peoples of Color throughout history so that I might feel like my experience was reflected through the past? Definitely. But the reality is that through the history discipline's dominant practices, queer Peoples of Color have been silenced and excluded from mainstream archives and narrative practices.

The purpose of this chapter is to set the disciplinary stage for why the forthcoming chapters are needed in the face of the dominant history discipline's failures. The chapter also sets the theoretical stakes beyond simple inclusion in the narrative, but rather a transformation of disciplinary inquiry through racial and ethnic community ways of knowing the past. I consider how queer Scholars of Color engage in historical inquiry, centering historical methods that arise from Queer of Color orientations toward the discipline. Building on Maribel Santiago's chapter, which grounds this book in a broader history of racial and ethnic communities asserting their own educational spaces, this chapter contextualizes how scholars from racially and ethnically marginalized communities engage and subvert the history discipline in the face of the discipline's failure to account for negated and erased communities.

Each of the following chapters follows a pattern of first providing context, then illustrating the specific community's approach to the past, and ending with implications for classroom practice. However, to set the theoretical stakes of the book, this chapter offers a deeper dive into how queer Scholars of Color engage with the history discipline to highlight its exclusionary norms and explore possibilities for theoretical interventions. This contrasts with the later chapters, which highlight approaches to the past that arise from within racial and ethnic communities and focus more on what these approaches might look like in classroom practice. I first contextualize Queer of Color approaches in relation to the history discipline and as an intervention into systems of domination today. This is followed by Queer of Color approaches to engaging history through erasure and negation, through disorientation, and as a horizon of future possibility. I then recount Queer of Color approaches to reading the archive. Finally, I consider practical implications for how these Queer of Color methods inform historical inquiry in the classroom to support students from historically marginalized communities.

CONTEXT: QUEER OF COLOR APPROACHES TO HISTORY

Incorporating queerness into the history curriculum is not as simple as adding content about queer people but instead requires engaging queerness as an approach to inquiry. Queer of Color engagements with history do not focus on more inclusive historical content about queer People of Color but consider the analytic practices that arise from communities at the intersection of queerness and racial marginalization. Queer of Color approaches to history involve confronting historical archives through negation, exclusion, and silence. This chapter considers how history classrooms might incorporate what queer People of Color do in the face of exclusion and negation.

Queer of Color approaches to one's own communities and knowledge formations often involve levels of disorientation and alienation within one's already marginalized communities. Although cultural knowledge and practices are frequently passed on by families within many ethnic and racial groups across generations, queer People of Color often grow up in isolation from one another, seeking out community and learning cultural knowledge, practices, and history from queer chosen family. An important aspect of Queer of Color approaches to history is that the term "queer People of Color" does not reflect a unified set of cultural and intellectual practices within a singular ethnoracial group. Although Queer of Color adds specificity to historical inquiry, it is a broad term that encompasses many localized communities expansive across time and space, and particular to distinct ethnic and racial groups' ways of knowing and being. As someone who works primarily in world history education, I understand the term "Queer of Color historical approaches" to encompass nonwhite peoples who resist colonialism and imperialism in addition to cisheteronormativity. Although I grew up identifying with my Japanese American family's history of being racially marginalized in the US, as I began teaching world history, I had to confront how my Japanese body represented Japanese colonialism and imperialism when viewed in a global context. Thus, every Queer of Color community and every queer Person of Color has their own particular relationship to the history discipline and what it means to do history.

A Queer of Color approach to history facilitates a constant critique and awareness of how power operates in one's ability to understand the past and its specter in the present. Once primarily used as a derogation to signal that which is strange or abnormal, the term *queer* today connotes a critique of how the category of *normal* is used to dominate and subordinate forms of difference in society. Queer theory's roots in performance studies link queerness to reading practices for analyzing how power functions and circulates.[1] Queerness is an analytic countermove to shift one's perspective beyond status quo identities. In history, a queer engagement with the past enables a critical lens toward the dominant society today, calling into question the identity of the categories and narratives one takes as given and natural. In this sense, queerness aligns with the historiographic aim of removing oneself enough from one's current situation to view the past and present from a new perspective along a critical horizon.

Enacting Queer of Color approaches to history cannot be incorporated through an additive approach; teachers must be willing to be self-reflective about how they are positioned within systems of power in society and in the classroom. Educators who want to teach history through Queer of Color approaches must take caution against cultural appropriation and misrepresentation or exoticizing Queer of Color communities. Queer Communities of Color have long experienced a history of cultural appropriation, such as the cooptation of Black and Latinx queer voguing balls in popular culture and media without adequate material compensation. Educators must be able to recognize the exclusionary practices embedded within the history discipline, their role as history teachers in reproducing such exclusionary practices, and appreciate Queer of Color approaches to the past as critical interventions into a problematic discipline.

APPROACHES TO THE PAST

Queer of Color History as Intervention

This chapter accounts for how students' racialized and queer experiences inform their engagement with history, in contrast to approaching historical thinking as a universal process indifferent to the role of race and identity. Engaging history from a position of marginalization involves not simply using the past to affirm present identities but exploring the relationship between identity and difference through historical inquiry. Applying Queer of Color methods to historical inquiry encourages students to be skeptical of finding themselves reflected in the past. This requires confronting the tension between one's present context and identity versus people's understandings of themselves in the past. Queer of Color approaches to history are liberatory practices in the face of intersecting systems of oppression today. Queer of Color scholarship allows one to be oriented to historical inquiry through one's experiences of alienation and marginalization.

Historical inquiry is personalized and particular, resulting from the encounter between the past and one's contemporary experiences within interwoven systems of power. Many philosophers of history frame this encounter as one between identity and difference, between the identity of the historian's present context and the difference of the past.[2] Queer People of Color exist in a contemporary American context in which they are generally at odds with the dominant identities of societal norms, experiencing the world through difference. Within historical inquiry, alienation can be an important tool for distancing oneself from one's context to gain a certain objectivity, to see the difference between a past historical moment and one's present lived reality. Sam Wineburg explained, "To realize history's humanizing qualities fully[,] . . . we need to encounter the distant past—a past less distant from us in time than in its modes of thought and social organization. It is this past, one that initially leaves us befuddled[,] . . . that we need most if we are to achieve the understanding that each of us is more than the handful of labels ascribed to us at birth."[3] Wineburg highlighted the important role that distancing plays in providing perspective on the limits of labels that box us in today. Queer People of Color's experiences of difference, although alienating, can become an asset within historical inquiry, intervening in the givenness of today's narrowly defined identity categories and dominant systems of oppression.

When one has been pushed to the margins of society, one has a particular vantage point for observation and analysis. Applying Queer of Color approaches to history must not reproduce alienation but value the alienation students already go through as an asset to students' historical inquiry. Queerness and Queer of Color approaches to history tap into this historiographic tension between identity and difference to expose the power of identity categories in the present through the queer difference of the past. In a previous study asking students if the ancient Egyptians were Black, it was a queer lesbian Student of Color who astutely asserted that the ancient Egyptians probably had their own way of identifying people beyond the racial categories we use today. This student expressed the importance of contextualization, which for me, as a queer Person of Color, is heightened by my own need to constantly recontextualize myself for those who might misread my sexuality and/or race.[4]

A Queer of Color engagement of history disorients us from the identity of the present, destabilizing its normative power over us. For example, when I teach about third-gender categories across various societies, it can at first sound strange and exotic to some students (and teachers). But by using a Queer of Color approach, I encourage students to flip the lens back toward our present condition, destabilizing the gender binary students have internalized as normal, and find fascination in the oddity and unique limitations of our contemporary gender roles and categories.[5] Queer of Color scholarship transforms history into a future horizon out of an oppressive present context, allowing one to dare to imagine the world otherwise. This chapter brings forth Queer of Color historians to incite educators toward incorporating students' queer and racialized experiences into their teaching of historical thinking skills. The need to intervene in the history discipline's dominant narratives of identity and difference is examined further in Jocyl Sacramento and Lauren Arzaga Daus' chapter, which offers a model for how educators might disrupt students' prior relationship to history through community-based relational practices of knowledge-sharing about the past.

Engaging History Through Erasure and Negation

I frame Queer of Color approaches to history as grounded in Roderick Ferguson's Queer of Color critique, which "addresses minority cultural forms as both within and outside canonical genealogies, pointing to the ruptural possibilities of those forms."[6] Queer of Color approaches to history are multiple and particular yet share common threads across approaches. Queer of Color critique does not arise from any singular ethnoracialized community, but from overlapping practices and traditions by LGBTQIA2S+ peoples across racial and ethnic communities. María Lugones addressed this tension between the overarching categorization of queer People of Color alongside the rich specificity beyond reductive categories. For Lugones, the tendency to categorize and classify is linked to colonial desires to make sense of the "other" by subsuming differences under Western scientific methods. "The logic and systems of oppression use categories and categorial logic because doing so fits the classifying, warehousing, and fragmenting of people."[7] Lugones explained further, "The logic of categories reduces and fragments, but it also conceals people as complex resistant beings that have lively histories."[8] Queer of Color approaches to history involve the intersectional erasures and silences produced through traditional history's norms and appreciates the agency within queer of Color communities to develop novel reading practices and historical methods in the face of erasure and negation.

Queer of Color approaches to history engage what history has done and continues to do with/to queer Peoples of Color. For Michael Hames-García and

Ernesto Javier Martínez, "Re-membering asks us to bring together a coalitional body that has been dis-membered by a history of ideological violence. In actively resisting that history of violence we are able not only to remember a history of conflict and coalition but also to re-member possibilities for collaboration in the present."[9] Queer Scholars of Color confront traumatic legacies of erasure and violence amid their present state of societal violence and negation. Queer Scholars of Color use historical inquiry to work through and beyond those traumatic legacies.

Rather than dismiss or sidestep the material absence of queer People of Color in the archive, many queer Scholars of Color inquire into that space of absence, negation, and erasure. Given the Orientalist portrayal of gay Asian men as passive, disempowered bottoms and objects acted upon, Nguyen Tan Hoang rearticulated the notion of bottomhood as capacious, attentive to coalitional social bonds with others rather than through relations of domination and subservience.[10] Darieck Scott considered abjection at the intersection of Blackness and queerness, and what else might be there in that space of abjection, through that relationality of negation.[11] Such Queer of Color scholarship brings Frantz Fanon's psychosocial concern for the negation of being Black in a white supremacist world in conversation with queer theory's embrace of failure as freedom to not reproduce the status quo.[12] A racial or ethnic community's experiences of erasure can become productive starting points for engaging with history. Both Muna Saleh and Meredith L. McCoy's chapters offer educational strategies for working through the traumatic legacies of the history discipline's exclusion and erasure of Palestinians and Native Americans, respectively.

For educators, I stress caution, but perhaps even more so, I want to stress awareness. Although many queer Scholars of Color have found engaging history's erasures and negations head-on to create something fruitful, it is not okay to require students from ethnically and racially marginalized communities to engage traumatic pasts. Instead, one might create openings and opportunities for such engagements if students wish to pursue them and be attentive to students' interests as they arise and shift at any given moment. Thinking back to my own experience in ninth grade, I might not have wanted to out myself by studying queer people during the Holocaust, but I was queerly drawn to studying artists deemed degenerate. My queerness might not have been apparent to my teacher, but the opportunity to explore my own line of inquiry enabled an engagement with history that I only later recognized as queer.

Engaging History Through Disorientation

Queer of Color approaches to history aim not to reify identities in the present but to disrupt the givenness of the categories one accepts as normal and universal today. The negation and erasure of queer People of Color within history enables a mode of historical inquiry grounded in alienation. This alienation reveals that the dominant categories used to make sense of people in society are insufficient. Queer Scholar of Color José Muñoz framed this alienation as *disidentification*, "descriptive of the survival strategies the minority subject practices in order to negotiate a phobic majoritarian public sphere that continuously elides or punishes the existence of subjects who do not conform to the phantasm of normative citizenship."[13] When the dominant identity categories negate and erase how one understands oneself, one disidentifies from such systems of categorization.

When one is alienated from normative forms of history, one is able to engage history from a different position that offers objective freedom from reproducing the status quo of the history discipline. Sara Ahmed's work on queer phenomenology emphasized the importance of allowing where one is located to orient oneself toward the object of study. There is a potential for a different historical objectivity within how queer People of Color are both oriented toward and disoriented through history, which can enable one to break away from history's seductive teleology of progress. Embracing the disoriented position of queer People of Color within history can offer objectivity through alienated subjectivity. Simultaneously, Queer of Color approaches to history enable critiques of our lived condition, using history to destabilize the status quo power over our lives. In a short film created by New York City queer Youth of Color in the afterschool program SupaFriends, the students juxtaposed historical footage of Puerto Rican and Venezuelan trans activist Sylvia Rivera against their contemporary issues as queer Youth of Color, not to equate their experiences but to shatter the hold of oppressive systems on the queer Youth of Color today and begin to imagine new solutions for the future.[14]

History then becomes a portal out of an oppressive present state to imagine other realities. As Muñoz stated, "We are not yet queer."[15] Queerness is a future on the horizon. Queerness offers a prismatic lens that refracts rather than reflects. Holding that prismatic lens to the past refracts the present beyond the appearance of a singular universal condition, opening a multiplicity of possibilities for being in the world. When one realizes that people in the past made sense of themselves and their worlds differently than we do today, one might see beyond the givenness of systemic racism, cisheteronormativity, and inequality today. For Muñoz, queerness utilizes "the past and the future as armaments to combat the devastating logic of the world of the here and now."[16] Instead of leading one to wallow in the victimhood of interlocking systems of oppression, Queer of Color approaches to history embrace disorientation as a means to challenge oneself and disrupt the perceived inevitability of the hegemonic status quo today. For educators, that alienation and disorientation can often lead students to dislike history, and that is OK. Educators must allow historical inquiry from each student's position and affective orientation and find ways to facilitate inquiry through such orientations. In chapter four, Brittany Jones and colleagues encourage educators to embrace the full spectrum of emotionality in Black people in the past and students in the present, including rage.

Engaging History as Horizon of Possibility

Queer of Color approaches to history extend a socially contextualized historiography as expressed by Hans Georg Gadamer. The alienation experienced by queer People of Color increases one's awareness that history is not neutral, enabling one to engage history fully aware of how one's own context is different from that of peoples in the past. This chapter's title plays on Gadamer's notion of the fusion of horizons as a model of historical inquiry that contextualizes the historian in the present as well as peoples in the past. Gadamer's historiography required an attentive reading practice that "involves neither 'neutrality' in the matter of the object nor the extinction of one's self, but the conscious assimilation of one's own fore meanings and prejudices. The important thing is to be aware of one's own bias so that the text may present itself in all its newness and thus be able to assert its own truth against one's own fore-meanings."[17] Gadamer understood history's potential to disrupt the givenness of one's current condition and the necessity of bypassing the allure of seeing oneself reflected in the past. Gadamer's approach encourages educators not to ask students to set aside their identities and unique interpretations grounded in their own contexts but instead asks students to recognize the difference between everything that text conveys within its own world and context alongside everything the student knows and understands within theirs. Gadamer does not ask the student to be unbiased but rather to be aware of how their own biases interact with what the text says in its own context. This also means that each student's encounter with a historical text and their interpretations and analyses will be unique because each student's context is unique, filled with their own experiences and identities. As a teacher, I must not only listen for the correct historical interpretation as defined by the state exam or standards but remain open to how students' experiences and identities inform their historical analysis, even when different from my own.

Queer Black scholar Nadia Ellis engaged Gadamer's notion of a fusion of horizons to consider how those within the Black diaspora approach the past to imagine new horizons into the future beyond the reproduction of racism's violence in the present. Nadia Ellis asserted that "wherever there is an outside, a possibility for difference, there is also a perception of the insufficiency of one's present circumstances."[18] How might educators enable an engagement with history through difference that calls into question the limits of one's present world order?

Queer of Color scholarship also embraces a critical humility that sits alongside utopian futures. Kadji Amin's archival inquiries underscored the notion of "living with damage in a damaged world," confronting unsavory truths about queerness within the archive.[19] Amin's queer mode of historical inquiry "calls for an acknowledgment of the 'complex personhood' of queer, racialized, and subaltern persons too often assigned the psychically flat role of righting the ills of an unjust social order and denied the right to be damaged, psychically complex, or merely otherwise occupied."[20] Amin pushes historical inquiry in the classroom to move beyond seeking redemption in the past to embrace both the complexity and damage within our current world order and within traces of the past.

Queer People of Color engage the archive through experiences within hegemonic systems of oppression, yet that engagement is not a means for recovering full subjectivity and redemption in the past. Rather, that encounter is a means to confront lingering traumas and hauntings of the past respective of one's full subjectivity in the present. Christina Sharpe worked through the past in light of her dual notions of the *wake*, in part as the haunting repercussions of the Atlantic slave trade, and *care*, as a means of attending to and healing from residual traumas.[21] For racially marginalized groups, there is a need to confront and acknowledge the reverberations of the past on the present. This requires acknowledging traumas in the present that result from that past and caring for how the wake of the past impacts people's lives in the present. For Sharpe,

> The ongoing state-sanctioned legal and extralegal murders of Black people are normative and, for this so-called democracy, necessary; it is the ground we walk on. And that it *is* the ground lays out that, and perhaps how, we might begin to live in relation to this requirement of our death. What kinds of possibilities for rupture might be opened up? What happens when we proceed as if we *know* this, antiblackness, to be the ground on which we stand, the ground from which we attempt to speak, for instance, an "I" or a "we" who know, an "I" or a "we" who care?[22]

Sharpe's engagement with the past does not lead one to be mired in the traumatic reverberations of history but enables possible ruptures of our present condition into the possibility of something else. Eliana Castro and Krista L. Cortes's chapter emphasizes AfroIndigenous practices of healing through historical inquiry, directly engaging students' past negative experiences and relationships with history through healing.

Knowing one's student population is important here. In order to center students' relationships to history, history classrooms must shift away from mere content memorization to give students opportunities to express their relationships to the world and to history and how the wake of history impacts them and those around them. This also requires educators to be self-aware and attentive to how inquiries into the past can be traumatic and/or enable one to heal from traumatic legacies of past injustices.

Queer of Color Reading Practices of the Archive

This section considers how Queer of Color historians cultivate novel reading practices of the archive. For the most part, Queer of Color historians encounter the archive just as any historian would, enacting historical thinking skills of sourcing, contextualization, and corroboration.[23] However, when the traces of queer People of Color have been erased or excluded from the archive, Queer of Color historians must cultivate reading practices that confront such absence and erasure. These novel practices challenge conventional disciplinary practices, placing Queer of Color historians at risk of being alienated from the history discipline. Emma Perez explained, "A historian must remain within the boundaries . . . as it has been conceptualized if she/he is to be a legitimate heir to the field. . . . Going outside the accredited realm of historiography means daring to be dubbed a-historical."[24] To queer is to offer a sustained critique of how power functions, including how power functions to regulate the norms of the discipline itself.

For example, consider the intersectional erasure of Black and trans American history. C. Riley Snorton confronted a "discarded archive" that often does not exist, with mere fragments and ephemera of the past at best. Snorton had to innovate practices for engaging in the historical past beyond what traditional historiography afforded. Snorton shifted his understanding of the archive as an object to emphasize trans as a grammatical movement within inquiry. Snorton's study traced how the concepts of Black and trans "have been constituted as fungible, thingified, and interchangeable, particularly within the logics of transatlantic exchanges," emphasizing the transitive nature of both concepts.[25] Queer and trans theory call into question the stability of identity categories, disrupting queer and trans bodies in the past from being categorized as objects of study. Instead, the ephemeral nature of queer and trans bodies in the past call into question the faith in archival stability and the appearance of stable evidence within history. In studying Black and trans American history, the archive's foundational role in history is called into question for its inability to account for Black trans bodies of evidence in the past. Our desire for documented tangible things might invoke the appearance of stability at any given moment, but our understanding of the past is ultimately fleeting and ephemeral. This ephemeral grasping at the past is akin to Bruce VanSledright's appreciation for elementary history students' understanding that we cannot fully know the past, and that is OK.[26] Understanding the past as ephemeral further helps students to view the present as only temporary, enabling hope for something else in the future.

Queerness and transness disrupt the normative power of teleological narratives in the history discipline and challenge the dependence on a linear chronology of history. For Snorton, "history becomes less a program for examining change over time and more an examination of disruptions in linear time."[27] For queer and trans People of Color in America, the state of violence and emergency is not the exception but the rule. Snorton begins his book by highlighting the current pattern of Black and trans individuals who have been violently murdered yet largely ignored by the state. Within the state's progressive linear narrative, any recorded moment of violence against Black and trans lives becomes framed as an exception, a mere moment of emergency within society's sustained forward progress. Snorton explained, "A *real* state of emergency occurs as a rupture in history to reveal" a state of emergence "in which the event of struggle challenges" history's commitment to a progressive ordered notion of time.[28] Tracing the legacies of violence and erasure toward Black and trans people disrupts history's teleological narratives of progress. For Snorton, this tracing does not reproduce these legacies but creates a rupture within history's progressive narrative, opening possibilities for something else to emerge. Queer and trans Scholars of Color engage history to work through the traumatic legacies of the past in hopes of emerging into something else.

For many Queer of Color historians, the seduction of finding one's heritage and legitimacy in the archive is a false one, given the absence of documentation. Instead, Anjali Arondekar proposed "a reading practice that redirects attention from the frenzied 'finding' of new archival sources to an understanding of the processes of subjectification made possible (and desirable) through the very idiom of the archive."[29] Arondekar's approach to the archive is not a means to recover Queer of Color subjects in the past but calls into question what traditional methods of history promise through archival research. Linked to Snorton's work, queer People of Color engaging the archive cannot hope to find themselves revealed in the archive, as one will primarily find voids and ephemera. But that inquiry into the archive can allow new inquiries into history's reliance on the archive to reveal subjects and bodies of evidence in the past. Arondekar recognized the false promise of what gets deemed as legitimized historical methods on behalf of empiricism. For Arondekar, "The critical challenge is to imagine a practice of archival reading that incites relationships between the seduction of recovery and the occlusions such retrieval mandates."[30] Building on Snorton's turn to trans as a grammatical relationship with the archive, Arondekar engaged the archive not as an object but as a means for revealing history's problematic methods that occlude through promises of revelation. In the classroom, the focus of inquiry shifts from getting students to find the right answers through the archive to getting them to question the limits of history's methods to provide complete pictures and voices of those in the past. Realizing that queer People of Color might not be legible in the archive does not have to be disappointing, but allows one to engage history differently, to be grounded not in the failure of those in the past to make themselves legible, but in history's failures to retrieve those from the past. For example, when teaching about African history, I have ninth-grade students read about how much of Africa's historical and archaeological past remains understudied, not because there is no history there, but because funding for research from Western institutions often determines which historic sites are worthy of study.

For some queer Scholars of Color, historical inquiry moves from explaining what traces exist to considering, as Saidiya Hartman framed it, "the subjunctive and conditional" modes.[31] The traditional grammar of the archive relies on the existence of evidence as proof, as confirmation. In the face of archival voids and ephemera, Queer of Color historians rely on other grammatical modes. The subjunctive mode expresses possibilities in the future, what might be rather than what is. The conditional mode also signifies what might be, under certain conditions.

Given Hartman's turn toward the subjunctive and conditional, some might view Hartman's work as fiction, outside the traditional history field's disciplinary boundaries. As Snorton and Arondekar sought historical methods to engage the archives through erasure and silence, Hartman's *Wayward Lives, Beautiful Experiments* bypassed the failures of history's disciplinary practices, to develop her own mode of inquiry through subjunctive and conditional modes of history. For Hartman,

> The intent of this practice is not to give voice to the slave, but rather to imagine what cannot be verified, a realm of experience which is situated between two zones of death—social and corporeal death—and to reckon with the precarious lives which are visible only in the moment of their disappearance. It is an impossible writing which attempts to say that which resists being said (since dead girls are unable to speak). It is a history of an unrecoverable past; it is a narrative of what might have been or could have been; it is a history written with and against the archive.[32]

Hartman begins with ephemera and traces surrounding the negative space where rebellious young Black women existed yet remain unaccounted for in the archive. She traces the settings and scenes where their lives took place, creating a novel form or archival study, producing a different kind of history. Beginning from archival photographs of alleyways and tenements, trial transcripts, and police reports, Hartman shifts the narrative possibility away from those who had the power to document, to imagine what the voices of Black rebellious women might have said, might have thought, might have done, despite what those in power documented. Hartman offers students and teachers a different model of historical inquiry and historical text and allows for different forms of engaging the pasts of those unretrievable through the archive.

Hartman is not alone in this move toward historical inquiry beyond the confines of the traditional discipline. Perez, while often recognized for her history monograph, engaged the past beyond traditional disciplinary forms through her novel *Gulf Dreams*, extending what historical inquiry can look like for those marginalized outside the formal boundaries of history. Perez's historical inquiries reflect the impossibility of fully recovering the Chicana/o subject through traditional history narrative methods. The Chicana/o subject in the past is either erased from the archive or inscribed by those who had the power to document, but rarely reflects the lives and thoughts of Chicanas/os in their own right. Perez reread the research on Chicana/o history to expose "how historians have participated in a politics of historical writing in which erasure—the erasure of race, gender, sexualities, and especially differences" was symptomatic of dominant narrative forms in the history discipline.[33] How might queer Scholars of Color dare to engage in historical inquiry inclusive of reimaginings of the past? How might we engage the past beyond the binary of fact and fiction? Perez and Hartman's works blur the lines between history and English classes, and they encourage cross-disciplinary collaborations between English and history teachers. Their works encourage cross-disciplinary conversations about narrative, contextualizing experiences and individuals, and the relationships between fiction and nonfiction texts. The afterschool program SupaFriends for queer trans Youth of Color in New York City serves as an example of what this subjunctive mode might look like in practice when students creatively engage the past to imagine possible futures.[34]

Engaging the past and archival work can also encourage history teachers to collaborate with the arts and art teachers. In a move to recover ephemera from historical oblivion, queer Chicana artist Guadalupe Rosales used an Instagram account *Veteranas y Rucas* to invite the public to share their images, creating a publicly created archive of Southern California's Chicanx communities. The archive includes photos from shopping mall portrait studios, as well as candid family photos. Rosales' archival project *Veteranas y Rucas* is not explicitly queer but is motivated by an urge to recover archives of communities formerly disregarded. This archival example reflects the theme of history as a process evidenced throughout this book (for example, in M. Yianella Blanco and Saleh's chapters). Rosales's project is not complete but is an ongoing process of community interaction and remembrance. Such examples express tenuous relationalities to the past and push beyond the history discipline's control over what doing history is supposed to look like. Such interdisciplinary examples also broaden the horizon of what historical inquiry can look like, engaging a broader range of student interests, learning modalities, and positionalities. Blanco's chapter offers another form of archival engagement through *testimonios* that emphasizes the collective process as transformative and results in the creation of new archival material.

IMPLICATIONS FOR PRACTICE: QUEER OF COLOR METHODS IN THE HISTORY CLASSROOM

If you are a queer Person of Color reading this, you might let this chapter give you permission to model what reading and inquiry can look like in your particular communities. Otherwise, you might consider how to cultivate an openness toward students' queer expressions, beyond what one assumes a queer identity and engagement to look like. Just as there is no one way that queer People of Color approach history, there is no single best way to engage queer Students of Color in historical inquiry, nor how to engage all students in history through Queer of Color practices. Queer of Color approaches to history allow unconventional spaces to meander and veer and change, despite mandated tests and disciplinary norms. Sometimes this might involve following queer Students of Color away from history, possibly into things like science fiction (like Octavia Butler's engagements of traumatic histories through science fiction).[35]

Through this chapter, my hope is to make educators more aware of the complex ways that queer People of Color choose to approach historical inquiry on their own terms and to be open to how one's own students might relate to history now and in the future. Sometimes, looking into the past can be healing, while other times, it can be traumatic. My hope is that educators remain attentive to how their own students might want to or not want to look into the past and to listen and attend to how students are already oriented to history. As an educator, my aim to make that act of looking into the past is not to reproduce traumatic narratives into the future, but to disrupt the legacies of systems of oppression in students' lives.

I also hope educators learn to recognize community forms of knowledge in their students beyond traditionally defined academic skills and beyond a mere engagement activity at the start of class. As evidenced earlier, there can be something plentiful and wildly nourishing within the disorientation and alienation that comes with being Queer of Color. One might consider how to engage students' funds of disorientation and alienation as productive entry points to historical inquiry away from the traditional discipline. I know that for myself in high school, I would have resisted directly engaging content that was explicitly Queer of Color for fear of being outed, but I would have welcomed content that engaged the strange, weird, and alien, the silenced and erased and misunderstood through traditional archival practices and approaches to history.

PART TWO

Thinking Holistically

CHAPTER 3

Expecting Indigenous Presence: Indigenous Pasts, Presents, and Futures in K–12 Social Studies

MEREDITH L. McCOY, TURTLE MOUNTAIN OJIBWE DESCENT

Sometimes, I feel like a scratched record, skipping to repeat the same measures of music over and over again. The audio itself is there, but the listener can't make sense of it. This metaphor, if you'll allow me to carry it a bit further, reveals two problems: the behaviors that led to the skipping in the first place (whether dust in the machine or scratches on the disk) and the unfulfilled but persistent desire of a frustrated listener demanding an experience.

This metaphor reflects the United States' inability to hear Indigenous voices, a problem reflected in the bodies of knowledge that history classrooms typically center. Indigenous people become the unintelligible sounds, even as we face the insatiable demand for our knowledges and stories. We create books and podcasts and lesson plans and curricula and teacher resources and policy briefs and, and, and . . . again and again; the listener rarely chooses to receive the message. This is no accident and little fault of Indigenous advocates: narratives of Indigenous disappearance, or at least Indigenous palatability, are forms of social control to maintain the status quo.[1] Narratives that essentialize, minimize, and erase Indigenous resistances to settler colonialism uphold the perceived righteousness of the state—and, therefore, are a core part of how the United States records its history.

We perpetuate these narratives in K–12 contexts, where textbooks, standards, and other resources have long failed to represent Indigenous people as contemporary, whole, and complex.[2]

Educators who think and write about Indigenous histories for K–12 classrooms, as well as the families whose students are represented in them, have been issuing calls for shifts in curricular representations and teacher behavior for at least the last hundred years. As a historian, I have seen these calls erupt from the archives, with Native parents and educators fighting schools, school boards, and state departments of education for shifts in public schools since at least the 1920s and in federally run and funded schools for much longer. These repeating calls have often fallen on unwilling ears, ears made unwilling to listen by their dysconsciousness—their internalized colonial misconceptions and related resistance to knowing otherwise—even as they may believe themselves willing to shift, listen, and learn.[3] They, too, often are limited by their own preconceived notions of Indigenous people, and their preconceptions prevent them from comprehending Native people as full, real, and whole. The stereotypes that shape the behavior of teachers, administrators, and other school staff, in turn, create real conditions of material harm for Native children and families as schools continually police Native children's bodies and minds.

This repeated refusal to give up assumptions about Native people (even by those who perceive themselves as willing to learn) reduces the capacity for schools and society to meaningfully change. "Good intentions" framing often covers up this unwillingness to learn while maintaining an image of benevolent support. This still causes harm, even if it is a different form of harm than overt physical or verbal violence. It also keeps us hoping that teachers and administrators will shift in their behavior, and we, in the spirit of believing in the potential for change, continue to provide our energy to support their growth. And we are often disappointed, as changes are ephemeral, superficial, or tokenized.

Teaching about Native people is never simple—the very fact of our continued existence undermines the imagined permanence and inevitability of the state as it is, and our communities, lifeways, and knowledges speak to other possible futures and social formations.[4] So before you continue, I'm asking you to stop and reflect on these preconceptions. Do you recognize your existing beliefs about who Native people are? Do you notice in yourself an unwillingness to listen beyond aspects of Indigeneity that affirm your current expectations? You cannot shift classroom practice for learning about Native people unless you are actively willing to confront your own beliefs about Native people. None of us are exempt from this—not white educators, not educators who are people of color, and sometimes not even other Indigenous educators (I certainly count myself among those continually fighting the insidious ways that simplified narratives about Native people creep into our minds and the curriculum).

CONTEXT

In this chapter, I argue for instruction about Native histories, presents, and futures that advances Eve Tuck's call to move beyond binaries of victimry and romanticization toward a more holistic and complex engagement with Indigenous life.[5] My approach to this work comes from my own life experience: first, as a former K–12 student who grew up in a mixed household with my Native dad and white mom, with some teachers who saw me as my full Turtle-Mountain-and-white self and with some teachers who could not; second, as a former K–12 educator who worked in social studies and English classrooms; and finally as a researcher who straddles American studies, history, Indigenous studies, and education in identifying histories of state violence and Indigenous resilience in schools.[6]

This chapter is about developing a habit of *expecting Indigenous presence*, a somehow still radical approach that upends settler narratives of Indigenous death and disappearance. Here, "presence" refers to the holistic, complicated, large- and small-scale, everyday stories of Indigenous people, both in response to and entirely separate from histories of colonial violence. My fervent hope is that, in helping your students learn to expect Indigenous life, they will become adults who are ready to hear messy, complex, and whole stories of Indigenous people, past, present, and future.

Before you read further, you should know that this chapter will not offer you insights into Indigenous spiritual traditions or other intimate knowledges; you do not need access to our teachings to teach about us ethically and appropriately (if that's why you're here, you might ask yourself what ideas you have about Native people that make you want such knowledge). Rather, I'm going to ask you to use already available Indigenous-created resources, including oral histories, blogs, and children's books, to center Indigenous voices and experiences in your classrooms. The strategies you will see here apply to educators of all backgrounds as you work with both Native and non-Native students. The work of shifting society to do right by Native people cannot be shouldered by Native people alone—it must fall on everyone.

APPROACH TO THE PAST: EXPECTING INDIGENOUS PRESENCE

Expecting Indigenous presence is a practice, one that extends beyond the absorption of historical information as it blends the traditionally stark lines between studies of history, studies of the present, and speculations on the future. It goes beyond an extractive approach of selecting Indigenous stories that emphasize decay or that focus solely on historical (but often tragic or isolated) Indigenous heroes. Instead, it asks for an integration of Indigenous knowledges throughout the curriculum such that students become surprised if Indigenous perspectives are not present. As such, expecting Indigenous presence does not fall neatly into a form of historical inquiry; it is a habit of mind, a developing of students' instincts as learners. In expecting Indigenous presence, students commit to developing a nagging sense in their brain whenever they see Indigenous communities *not* represented in their classrooms, one that makes them stop and ask for the rest of the story. In conversation with anticolonial literacy and Ashley Cordes and Leilani Sabzalian's call for critical Indigenous literacies, expecting Indigenous presence encourages students to expect representation of the Indigenous voices too often made invisible within the curriculum, the textbook, and their class discussions.[7]

Expecting Indigenous presence unsettles the status quo by asking students to recognize stories of Indigenous persistence in the face of genocide. These may be conversations about Indigenous resistance, but they may also be conversations about the everyday ways that Indigenous people continue to be ourselves through the persistence of our languages, lifeways, value systems, and connections to place and one another. This is a stark redirection from the kind of cherry-picked, hero-centered narrative students typically receive, one where the primary Indigenous figures (Pocahontas and Sacagawea, for example) are presented relative to a replacement myth of Indigenous extinction and the glorified establishment of white life on Indigenous lands.[8]

Given the existing stereotypes of Indigenous people as either savage warriors or romanticized heroes, it would be easy to conflate expecting Indigenous presence with expecting Indigenous resistance. This perhaps aligns with the oft-repeated phrase, "Our existence is resistance." There is a danger, however, in oversimplifying Indigenous people to only forms of political resistance. Doing so denies Indigenous people the same fullness and complexity afforded to other groups, as well as the right to rest and play. Expecting Indigenous presence instead extends to all forms of life: joy and play, art and creativity, conflict and struggle, relations with place and each other, dreams and possibility, frustration and disappointment. Our classrooms must be full of opportunities for students to see Indigenous people in all of these ways. The sum of these experiences is what makes us human.

Cultivating a practice of seeing Indigenous people as fully human, as fully complex, as fully present, and as fully relevant will shape how students interact with Indigenous people beyond the classroom. This feels so obvious and is such a low bar. And yet, the stakes could not be higher. We are in a moment of ever-accelerating climate change connected to an extractive capitalism that continually exploits and pollutes Indigenous bodies, lands, and waters. As of 2018, 80 percent of the world's remaining biodiversity persists in Indigenous-stewarded territories.[9] This statistic undoubtedly needs updating, given the raging deforestation of the Amazon and ongoing pipeline spills in Indigenous-stewarded territories. At the same time that colonial extraction has driven us to a boiling point, the United States continues its attacks on Indigenous individuals: Supreme Court cases threaten our rights to care for our children (as in the now-resolved *Haaland v. Brackeen*, which sought to undermine the Indian Child Welfare Act of 1978) and to generate our own forms of economic development (as in *Maverick Gaming LLC v. United States*). Federal agencies undermine our rights to care for our homelands through permissive regulations that favor oil companies over land protections. The prison system, K–12 school-based discrimination, and interpersonal forms of gender-based violence target and harm Indigenous individuals, families, and communities. To grow toward more just forms of relating to one another and to survive as human beings into the future, we need students to grow into informed adults who see Indigenous people not as obstacles to sidestep or as mythical figures constrained to the past but as contemporary partners in building a world in which we can all continue to live.[10]

This is a task that falls to all of us, though non-Native students and teachers undoubtedly have more to do when it comes to learning to see Indigenous life all around them. As educators, we can cultivate this practice with our students by working alongside them to center a wide range of Indigenous voices in the materials we choose. Indigenous content creators have made such resources abundant;

they critique the centuries of attacks on our languages, families, lands, and lifeways and celebrate our present and future possibilities through their podcasts, books, radio shows, TV series, films, music, curricular resources, journalism, museum exhibits, and Instagram, YouTube, and TikTok accounts, among so many others. Working with students to learn from these Indigenous-produced media can help students adjust to a practice of turning to Indigenous voices as valid and trustworthy sources.

IMPLICATIONS FOR PRACTICE

As I mentioned at the start of this chapter, Indigenous people have been demanding these kinds of shifts in schools since the imposition of colonial schooling on this continent. If it were so easy to shift mindsets about Indigenous people, including school-based narratives, perhaps it would have been done by now. And yet, a stubborn hope keeps us believing that shifts toward change are possible. Indigenous-created texts and strategies are increasingly available, and while there is always more to do, scholars have published ample examinations of what works and what does not in teaching Native topics in K–12 spaces.[11] As one of these scholars, I am not particularly special, nor do I have anything to offer that generations of other Indigenous leaders, scholars, and families have not already said. But, as a former social studies teacher, I will offer some of these strategies again here in the hope that you will commit to using them.

To sustainably develop teaching programs about Native issues, relationships with people and place must be at the center of teachers' and schools' practice.[12] While the kind of relationally and situationally specific guidance needed to build these relationships falls outside the scope of this chapter, scholars and nonprofits have issued materials offering guidance for ethical stances and tangible steps.[13]

Indigenous Visibility Inquiry

The remainder of this chapter now turns to an inquiry-based module with instructional strategies that teachers can engage in alongside their students to center Indigenous voices. In alignment with the C3 Framework's emphasis on inquiry, skills, and practices toward democratic decision-making, this module centers two compelling questions: "How can we seek out the histories that our existing narratives and resources make invisible?" and "How does our understanding of American society shift when Indigenous voices, stories, histories, and futures are part of the picture?" Both questions have implications that ripple out beyond social studies into the sciences, mathematics, and language arts, all areas where Indigenous histories, intellectual contributions, and political landscapes should shape classroom practice.

This module focuses on skills and resources at the high school level, with many texts appropriate to younger readers at a variety of reading levels. I have attempted to make the module flexible so that you can tailor it in light of your state's standards and the reading levels of your students.

This module can and should be stretched across the academic year. Indeed, it is critical that you not try to implement this module only during the month of November, as confining Indigenous histories and contributions to one month sends the implicit signal to students that it is appropriate to duck in and out of remembering Indigenous people. Rather, teachers and students together must shift toward seeing Indigenous people as relevant to all content all year long. Integrating these questions throughout the content areas and across the school year also helps with the ever-present pressures of time and standards.

Before you begin work with your students, a few notes on your own preparation: if you jump right into this content before doing your own homework, you could easily inflict new harms through a lack of knowledge or the projection of your own preconceptions about Indigenous people. Rather than taking this as a reason to avoid Indigenous topics altogether, do some research. Read a book like Paul Chaat Smith's *Everything You Know about Indians is Wrong* or Anton Treuer's *The Heartbeat of Wounded Knee.* Follow Indigenous content creators on social media. Subscribe to Indigenous news outlets like indianz.com, Indian Country Today, nativenews.net, or Native America Calling. Learn which Indigenous nations claim the lands and waters where you live (a website like native-land.ca is one place to start) and visit their websites to educate yourself about pressing contemporary issues and how their governments operate today. Know which Native-run nonprofits operate in your area. Be transparent with your students if this is new information to you, and bring them along with you in your own learning process.

Part I: Undoing Myths and Stereotypes

Any engagement with Indigenous histories first requires identifying and unlearning the myths and stereotypes teachers and students carry about Indigenous peoples. Using the supporting question—"How do myths or stereotypes make it harder to see people as they are?"—examine the website for the National Museum of the American Indian's exhibit *Americans.*[14] As you and your students see the overwhelming number of items using inaccurate, stereotypical images of Indigenous people, have them journal or discuss the impact of being surrounded by inaccurate representations of a group of people. Journal alongside them, thinking about your own mindsets and growth. How do these representations keep non-Native people from seeing Native people as they are? And what might the impact of this be for Native people? To take this a step further, look together at Tulalip scholar Stephanie Fryberg's excellent research on the impacts of mascots on Indigenous youth, which found that even Native youth who did not believe themselves to be impacted by stereotypical images demonstrated lower self-confidence and a lower sense of community worth after viewing such images.[15] As an extension, depending on the age of your students, you might also learn more about the harms of mascots' stereotypical imagery in films like *Imagining the Indian* or *More than a Word.*

Once you have examined how stereotypes perpetuate myths about Native people, read excerpts of the young people's edition of Anton Treuer's *Everything You Wanted to Know about Indians but Were Afraid to Ask.*[16] Working through Treuer's book together can model for your students the importance of identifying and unlearning inaccurate narratives about other groups of people. In addition, you can use this book to frame how you and your students will prioritize contemporary Indigenous voices from a variety of nations throughout the year as you learn to expect Indigenous presence. To help students recognize Indigenous diversity, start a classroom list of Indigenous people you are learning from throughout the year—you already have three: Paul Chaat Smith (Comanche), an essayist and the curator of the *Americans* exhibit; Stephanie Fryberg (Tulalip), a researcher and professor; and Anton Treuer (Ojibwe), an author and professor.

As you wrap up this first section, return to the question, How do myths or stereotypes make it harder to see people as they are? Tailor the task to your students with these few (out of many) possibilities: a brief reflection essay that cites specific examples from your class discussions and resources, an art piece that reflects on how stereotypes reinforce narratives that benefit the status quo, or another exercise that addresses local stereotypes, particularly, but not necessarily exclusively, for Native people. Complete one of these exercises alongside your students as you continue to model for them your own commitment to continual learning.

Part II: Using Existing Resources

Teachers and students often demonstrate a learned helplessness when it comes to Native content. And yet, Native educators, artists, writers, and government leaders (among others!) have already offered resources to educate non-Native people about our histories, life experiences, and plans for the future. Building on your engagement with Anton Treuer's work and the ever-growing list of Native people you're learning from, name this learned helplessness and commit to educating yourselves by reading, watching, and listening to what Indigenous people already share about themselves, their histories, and their dreams.

This emphasis on what Indigenous people share *voluntarily* and *publicly* is important. Native people have been fighting the over-surveillance of our families and communities since the advent of colonialism.[17] Focusing on the materials that Native people have chosen to curate or create for other people can help students learn to respect that some information is for everyone, while other information may be private or specific to certain groups.

In accessing these public materials, have students move through three focus areas: marking connections to place; governance, leadership, and social change; and recounting histories. Taken as a whole, these three focus areas connect to standards for geography, civics, and history and offer ways to see Indigenous people in past, present, and future contexts.

Marking Connections to Place

As constructed materials, maps both reflect and reinforce cultural beliefs about places, values, and other people. This dive into mapping can help students upend the idea that there is only one way to do mapping and look more critically at the messages that maps communicate about places and the people who move in them. These are human-produced documents whose origins should be as much a part of classroom analysis as the content of the maps themselves. Each of the following resources helps students think about the purpose of maps beyond finding directions—how do maps encode information about what we value, about our connection to place, and about our histories and futures there?

After discussing the need to rethink maps, turn toward Indigenous cartographies. For a brief overview, watch the five-minute cartography episode of PBS's *Indigi-Genius*, led by Laguna Pueblo educator and comic book creator Lee Francis IV.[18] Then, take a look at recent Indigenous mapping projects like Mapping Indigenous LA, Indigenous Chicago, or the Bdote Memory Map.[19] With your students, think about how these maps differ from the maps you're used to seeing. How do these maps represent a form of agency as Indigenous people represent themselves and their connections to place? How does this reorient how you think about space and place? What messages about Indigenous people are present in the maps you're used to seeing (including messages about Indigenous absence or invisibility) as compared to these Indigenous-created ones?

As you push disciplinary boundaries of what constitutes geographic knowledge, bring in Indigenous-created artwork. For example, compare a map, like Dakota artist Marlena Myles's map of the Twin Cities in Minnesota, with what appears on Google Maps.[20] This comparison offers a chance to assess what places we consider worth recording and how we record them, as well as analyze what components an image needs to be considered a "map." Take this a step further (and into the future!) by examining Myles's incorporation of geolocating and virtual reality in her Dakota Spirit Walk art installation.[21] What possible speculative futures are opened through such virtual reality mapping projects? How might mapping be a way to challenge the world as it is and imagine other presents or futures?

Finally, as a bridge with your science standards, look into the place-based exercises from the Learning in Places curriculum, led by Italian and Ojibwe scholar Megan Bang.[22] Consider how we are all actively participating in recording and understanding our shared spaces, as well as what our responsibilities to place are because of our relationships with each other, the lands and waters, and our more than human relations.

Governance, Leadership, and Social Change

Indigenous people are remarkably absent from most states' civics standards.[23] If this is true in your state, it does not have to keep you from addressing Indigenous models of governance and leadership. Knowing how people organize themselves politically is a crucial part of understanding the story we tell ourselves about who we are, as well as how we represent our communities to the world. Learning about

Indigenous models for governance and leadership can help you and your students connect to your civics standards regardless of whether they explicitly mention Indigenous people.

K–12 curriculum too often leaves teachers and students unaware of tribal sovereignty and unfamiliar with treaty histories. To build your and your students' background knowledge, begin with the Smithsonian's Native Knowledge 360 module on treaties in the Northern Plains.[24] Focus on treaties as formal, permanent, government-to-government agreements about how we interact with one another. Note that treaties *affirm* (but do not bestow) Native nations' inherent right to self-governance that precedes colonization and will persist into the future. Then, have your students join you in the research you completed before starting this module: work alongside them to learn about the current governance structures of the nations who claim your area within their traditional homelands and waters by looking at their websites and social media accounts. Where are their government offices located today? How do their tribal government website and social media describe their governing responsibilities and how they take care of their people? What story does the government's website and social media tell about its people and their history, present, and future?

Connecting with your standards for governance and social change, learn to look for Indigenous leadership. Native leaders serve in all levels of governance, including local municipal, state, federal, and tribal offices. With your students, select one or more books that profile Indigenous leaders, like the book on Minnesota lieutenant governor Peggy Flanagan (Ojibwe) in the Minnesota Humanities Center's *Native American Lives* series or the children's book *Sharice's Big Voice* about US representative from Kansas Sharice Davids (Ho-Chunk) by Davids and coauthor Nancy K. Mays.[25] How do these Indigenous-authored books talk about these Indigenous leaders? How does reading about the role of Indigenous leaders help us understand Indigenous presents, pasts, and futures? Why might children's books be an important avenue for learning (and teaching!) about Indigenous leadership?

Take a similar approach to learning about Indigenous leadership outside of American governance. Read Cherokee scholar Adrienne Keene's *Notable Native People* and Ojibwe scholar Katrina Phillip's annual Twitter feeds on Native women for Women's History Month to build an understanding of the breadth of Indigenous advocacy across time and topic. What shared strategies for social change do you notice? How are these Native people building stronger, healthier futures for their communities and across Indian Country?

As you think together about Indigenous-led social change, spotlight the role of journalists in representing ourselves and advancing important social issues. Zoom in on the Indigenous Journalists Association, and help students access Indigenous-authored media, such as the news outlets you checked in on before starting the inquiry module.[26] Together, make a plan for how you and your students might incorporate Native voices, including Native journalists, into your existing routines of learning about current events in the world.

Lastly, connect civics and artwork by learning about the photojournalism of Swinomish and Tulalip artist Matika Wilbur in Project 562.[27] Read about Wilbur's intentions for the project, and link this back to the first module activity on stereotypes—how does telling contemporary visual stories of Indigenous community members and community leaders shift the narrative about who Native people are?

Recounting Histories

For generations, Western knowledge systems have undermined the importance and value of oral traditions and oral histories. And yet, these sources are critical in how Indigenous people transmit value systems, shared histories, and local knowledges.[28] To understand the importance and value of oral histories, examine the United Nations Declaration on the Rights of Indigenous People (available in its original form and a version adapted for Indigenous teens) and talk together about the importance of Articles 13 and 31, both of which protect Indigenous oral histories and traditions.[29] Why do you and your students think such protections needed to be created? And what might the importance of safeguarding orally transmitted knowledge be for the future?

Indigenous forms of education prioritize intergenerational learning, often through stories shared by elders. For this dive into oral histories, you can access interviews that are publicly and freely available through multiple online sources. Given the frequent burden schools place on a small number of Indigenous elders and knowledge keepers, making use of these other resources can be a good place to start, particularly if your school doesn't yet have strong local relationships. Looking at your history standards, identify a particular topic or trend (like urbanization, treaty histories, or military history) and view clips from existing oral history archives such as North Dakota's Native American Essential Understandings and South Dakota's Oceti Sakowin Essential Understandings to grow your shared understanding of the topic.[30] Additional oral histories are embedded through the Smithsonian's Native Knowledge 360 exercises, which are searchable by topic. Engage these interviews as valid sources of knowledge that reflect individuals' memories and experiences. Avoid using written documents to "fact check" the oral histories and instead frame them as equally valuable complements to written sources that together can offer you all a richer picture of the history you're studying.

As you and your students talk about the importance of oral histories, remember that you have already been primed by previous school texts and media to hear "Indigenous oral traditions" and think of the over-simplified pourquoi tales (stories with titles like "How Did Rabbit Get His Tail"). While such stories can do important pedagogical work, they too often have been extracted from their social and linguistic contexts, resulting in versions far removed from their original moral, ecological, and political meanings. Moreover, many of these stories made their way out of the community and into publication through inappropriate extraction by anthropologists. Such stories are not part of this module. If you are committed to sharing books that include such stories, vet them carefully for ethics and for authorship. Find out whether Indigenous people were ethically involved in the process and remember that some stories have seasonal or gendered restrictions for telling.

Indigenous authors have written a number of books for children and young adults that reflect on historical topics that you can pair with the oral histories above. For example, if you choose to learn from the oral histories on Indigenous urbanization, you might also assign *Indian No More* by Charlene Willing McManis (Umpqua/Confederated Tribes of Grande Ronde) and Traci Sorell (Cherokee Nation), which tells the story of a young girl as her family navigates both relocation and their nation's termination by the federal government. For extensive, updated lists of Indigenous-authored historical fiction, see Nambé Pueblo scholar Debbie Reese's blog *American Indians in Children's Literature*, where she reviews children's books about Indigenous people, or Understand Native Minnesota's *A Guide to Reliable Native American-Related Teaching Resources*.

Help students see Indigenous people not just as part of the past but also as part of their local contemporary community. If available in your area, you might go with them to local Indigenous-run[31] or Indigenous-curated art galleries, museums, restaurants, or community events open to the public (check publicity materials to make sure the audience is open to everyone). How might you and your students use these experiences to move beyond learning toward committing to support Indigenous businesses and artists as members of your local community? With your students, journal or discuss how your understandings of Indigenous people change when you see them as members of your local community rather than figures of a historical past.

Wrapping it up: "How can we seek out the histories that our existing narratives and resources make invisible?" and "How does our understanding of American society shift when Indigenous voices, stories, histories, and futures are part of the picture?"

Over the year, you and your students are building habits of expecting Indigenous presence through more accurate and updated representations that confront colonial stereotypes and through Indigenous perspectives on mapping, social change, and history. Throughout this process, you've built a class list of Indigenous leaders to learn from and a practice of turning to Indigenous people as subject matter experts. By the end of the year, you and your students may be asking, "What next? Where do I/we go from here?"

If you and your students are interested in building toward informed action in support of Indigenous priorities, start again by doing your homework. While you may want to jump right in by inviting class visitors or taking your students out into the community, be wary of demands on Native people for their time, energy, or labor, particularly if your school does not yet have existing, mutually beneficial relationships. Read Leilani Sabzalian's book *Indigenous Children's Survivance in Public Schools,* particularly the chapters on school assemblies and collaborations with Native nations, for cautionary notes about how to proceed.

If you decide to take some informed action, start locally. Using your newly strengthened skills of listening to Indigenous journalists, content creators, government leaders, and activists, educate yourselves about currently pressing issues for Indigenous people in your area (including urban Native communities and any Indigenous refugees or relocatees from other parts of the world) and/or for the Native nations who may have been removed from the place where you live and learn. Much of the time, there are already social media posts and news stories sharing information and inviting the public to participate in specific ways, whether through fundraising, amplifying current messages, and/or sending supplies. Talk with students about the importance of respecting boundaries, following community priorities, and joining in where community members have said it would be appropriate (and welcomed!).

Throughout your research, implementation, and reflection on any informed actions you take, thread together your previous learning about Indigenous people—past, present, and future—from the rest of the year. Ground your reflections on Indigenous peoples' visions for the future as discussed publicly in art, social media, press releases, and protests. With your students, explore how this experience has changed how you collectively approach Indigenous histories.

Finally, as you wrap up the year, return to your original questions: "How can we seek out the histories that our existing narratives and resources make invisible?" and "How does our understanding of American society shift when Indigenous voices, stories, histories, and futures are part of the picture?" Reflect in writing, art projects, and class discussions on how your approaches to Indigenous knowledges have changed and, in the process, how your understanding of absent narratives and Indigenous peoples may change the approach each of you takes to learning in the future.

CLOSING THOUGHTS

The materials I've proposed here are only a small sliver of the many publicly available ways to support building a habit of expecting Indigenous presence. While colonial knowledge formation and Western schooling have long marginalized Indigenous perspectives and voices, shifts are possible that center Indigenous peoples' representations of their own lives, histories, and futures. These shifts transcend disciplinary and temporal boundaries, blurring the dividing lines between history, art, geography, political science, past, present, and future.

My hope for you and your students is that you develop habits of listening for Indigenous voices and that you refuse to accept Indigenous absence and stereotypical misrepresentations in available narratives, both in and out of school. Rather than allowing the skipping album to continue to skip, message unheard, I hope you will take on the work to slow down, clean your setup, and strengthen your ability to hear, learn, and amplify. Making shifts in classrooms to value Indigenous knowledges and expertise will require significant work from teachers and students alike, but such work is imperative for our collective health and well-being moving into the future.

CHAPTER 4

We Have Joy but What About Rage? An Examination of Race and Emotions

BRITTANY JONES, DAWNAVYN JAMES,
LAGARRETT J. KING, AND DAPHANIE BIBBS

No matter where we go, the most frequently asked question the Center for Black History and Racial Literacy Education at the University at Buffalo receives is about teaching Black history in elementary schools. Many questions focus on educational resources such as children's literature or about where to begin Black history instruction. According to many educators, teaching Black history is hard, but the teachers who experience the most difficulty are at the elementary level. The difficulties elementary teachers face are numerous, primarily stemming from a lack of Black history education at the K–12 level and their uncritical interrogation and acceptance of whiteness and anti-Blackness at post-secondary levels. Additionally, teachers fear being labeled as a racist or believe that Black history is too controversial or inappropriate for elementary students. Furthermore, even when Black history is included in classroom instruction, miseducation ensues because social studies standards and curricula present incomplete, decontextualized, and redundant narratives of Black history through Eurocentric lenses.[1] As a result, social studies curriculum materials often portray Black histories through a white gaze that oversimplifies and dehumanizes Black narratives.

In this chapter, we focus on how attending to Black people's emotions during Black history instruction can dismantle the miseducation and dehumanization perpetuated by subpar curriculum materials. Drawing on findings from a previous study, we argue that Black emotions are a necessary yet understudied aspect of Black history education. Although Black history curricula tend to focus on Black people's feelings of joy, hope, and determination, we assert that more attention must be given to emotions such as rage and anger. Attending to the full range of emotions that Black people have experienced throughout history can strengthen and humanize Black history education while simultaneously assuaging the harm and miseducation that occurs when curriculum materials present Black people as emotionless or as bodies only capable of feeling positive emotions.[2] In the following sections, we provide context through a brief literature review, a description of our conceptual frameworks, and information about our study. We then introduce Critical Analysis of Racialized Emotions (CARE), a framework educators can use to incorporate a critical analysis of emotions into their Black history instruction.

CONTEXT

It is no secret that Black history education is a struggle to implement in our nation's classrooms, but the absence of Black history in schools is concerning for several reasons. First, students suffer. Research has noted that Black history is instrumental in Black students' academic achievement, cultural socialization, and mental health.[3] Second, history has power and can influence how individuals conceptualize race relations and Blackness. Said differently, history influences how we understand other people's identities; therefore, what we learn about history is what we learn about people, not only in the past but also during contemporary times. Currently, most history education implies that Black people were problems to be solved and are rarely seen as problem solvers. They are seen as slaves who contributed little to democracy and were a drain of valuable resources. Black folks in history are seen as powerless, childlike figures, who were beholden to whiteness and relied on white people to gain access to society. Only a few topics, such as slavery, the Civil War, Reconstruction, the civil rights movement, and people like Martin Luther King Jr., Rosa Parks, and Harriet Tubman, are consistently featured in the curriculum.[4] These topics and people are essentially the only representation of Black history that students learn throughout their K–12 careers. When this miseducation happens, students are left with a contentious relationship with Black history because students learn little about Black people's humanity.[5]

Black History Instruction and Social Studies Standards in Elementary Classrooms

Apart from Black History Month, Black history is predominantly incorporated into elementary literacy curricula.[6] To complicate Black history instruction in elementary schools, scholars have encouraged educators to use children's literature to decenter whiteness within Black history instruction and to engage in discussions of race and racism.[7] According to Norline R. Wild, the illustrations and text within picture books allow children to see and understand Black people's emotions, experiences, and struggles, which helps students connect the experiences of the characters to their own lives while also gaining exposure to cultures and people that differ from them.[8] In addition to children's books, scholars have also studied how teachers use historical inquiry to guide students through nuanced narratives of enslavement, which can support all students' racial literacy development and can build students' racial identities.[9] While resources have been created to support teachers through the nuances of Black history education in elementary classrooms, elementary curricula still lack intentional implementation of Black histories throughout the school year.[10]

Even more, in states with Black history mandates, elementary social studies standards tend to focus on Black heroes or holidays.[11] For example, New York's social studies standards require kindergarteners to learn when and why national holidays, such as Martin Luther King Jr. Day, are celebrated to help "develop a shared culture and identity within the United States."[12] Although this standard aims to cultivate a shared cultural identity by focusing on the cognitive aspects of when and why MLK Day exists, we posit that a more critical approach should include the noncognitive, emotional aspects of Black history education.

Instead of solely teaching students the facts about MLK Day, educators should also address the emotions associated with it. For instance, educators could explain to their students that King's legacy of fighting for justice and equality cultivated emotions and feelings of hope and pride among people in the US, which led to the creation of MLK Day. Conversely, educators might teach their students that King was assassinated for fighting against injustice and racism, which cultivated emotions and feelings of guilt, sadness, or rage, leading to the creation of MLK Day. Both approaches not only offer explanations about why MLK Day was created, but by centering emotions, students are also able to understand how people's emotional responses to the legacies of historical figures and the celebration of holidays are inextricably linked. Additionally, because students might experience varied emotional responses when learning about why holidays were created, teachers could draw from these responses to ask students whether certain holidays should exist (e.g., Columbus Day). Teachers could also interrogate the standards by asking students: What does *a shared cultural identity* mean if we have different emotional responses to historical figures?

Effectively incorporating a critical discussion of emotions into Black history instruction, however, is challenging because many elementary teacher education programs rarely explore Black history in depth, let alone the emotional aspects of Black history. As such, many educators have little foundational knowledge about Black history. We recognize that educators may feel reticent or uncomfortable teaching about Black emotions, which could lead educators to (un)consciously reproduce harmful stereotypes about Black people—especially when discussing emotions such as rage or anger. Later in this chapter, we revisit this tension and provide educators with questions and cautions to consider when teaching through Black emotionality.

Conceptual Framings

Black Historical Consciousness. To help teachers teach Black history, King developed a Black history framework called Black Historical Consciousness, which Pitts and James adapted to connect with the elementary classroom (figure 4.1).[13] The Black Historical Consciousness framework consists of eight principles, which are centered on Black perspectives and Black cultural ways of knowing, doing, and long-standing traditions. The eight principles of the framework are: (1) Power, oppression, and anti-Blackness; (2) Agency, resistance, and justice; (3) Africa and the African Diaspora; (4) Black Emotionality; (5) Black Identities; (6) Black Historical Contention; (7) Black Social Histories; and (8) Black Futurism.

Racialized Emotions. Racialized emotions are the types of emotions produced when racialized people *feel* race within racialized societies.[14] Black emotions are a specific type of racialized emotions that are produced when Black people *feel* race within a racialized society. For example, when Black people experience anti-Black

FIGURE 4.1 Black historical consciousness for P–12

A PK-12 BLACK HISTORY FRAMEWORK

Black Historical Consciousness

DEVELOPED BY DR. LAGARRETT J. KING

Power, Oppression, & Anti-Blackness	Highlight the lack of justice, freedom, equality, and equity of Black people experienced throughout history.
Agency, Resistance, & Justice	Black histories that explain that although Black people have been victimized, they were not helpless victims.
Africa & the African Diaspora	African and African Diaspora as Black histories stresses narratives of Black people be contextualized within the African Diaspora.
Black Emotionality	Narratives that focus on Black people's emotions, including joy, fear, rage, sadness, and hope.
Black Identities	Black identities as Black histories is a more inclusive history that seeks to uncover the multiple identities of Black people through Black history.
Black Historical Contention	The recognition that all Black histories are not positive and pristine. It highlights humanity's messiness. Contention recognizes that all Black people do not hold similar views or support other Black people. Some even to the detriment of Black people's freedom and justice. We should recognize the not-so-great aspects of Black histories and that Black people have been guilty of all the isms and phobias that plague global societies.
Community Local, & Social Histories	Teaching Black history through "regular" persons who made a difference in their communities and state. This approach to history removes the messiah complex and may not be the most "popular" or "respectable" but those who fought for the everyday person.
Black Futurism	Using lessons from Black histories to reimagine the contemporary and future.

University at Buffalo
Center for K–12 Black History
and Racial Literacy Education

Source: LaGarrett J. King's Black Historical Consciousness Framework, adapted for the elementary classroom by Brianne Pitts and Dawnavyn James.

discrimination, the emotions they feel are a result of that anti-Black interaction and can only be experienced by people racialized as Black.[15] Nuanced understandings of Black emotionality, however, extend beyond mere recognition that Black people feel a multitude of emotions. To teach about Black emotionality and Black history effectively, educators and curriculum materials should make clear connections between Black emotions and Black agency. As Brittany L. Jones noted, Black emotions are agentic and subversive; they are historic while concurrently traversing history into the present, and they illuminate Black people's humanity while simultaneously revealing the perpetual dehumanization of Black people.[16]

Black emotions are at the core of Black experiences, but without a critical understanding and inclusion of Black emotions in history curricula and instruction, Black history education will always be incomplete. In our study, we drew from theories of Black emotions, specifically Black rage, to guide our literary analysis of the elementary textbooks.

Black Rage. Black scholars have offered a variety of definitions of Black rage and, to some extent, Black anger.[17] James Baldwin famously described Black rage as a consciousness of the anti-Blackness that is happening *around all* Black people *all the time.*[18] Cornell West argued that Baldwin's conception of rage is an expression of love for the Black community because one must love Black people to feel rage when Black people are treated unjustly.[19] Similarly, Bryan J. McCann contended that Black rage is an "affective dialectic between communal affinity and jarring encounters with injustice," which suggests that without love for Black people, Black rage cannot exist.[20] William H. Grier and Price M. Cobbs identified Black rage as an emotional response that arises when Black people "have been asked to shoulder too much."[21] These conceptions of Black rage should not be confused with aggression but rather understood as an emotional response that both recognizes the permanence of anti-Blackness and amplifies Black humanity by disrupting societal expectations that Black people should endure racial violence absent of emotional responses.[22]

The racialized emotions that Black people feel are a consequence of living in a society created and maintained by racial hierarchies. Although we focus specifically on Black rage in this chapter, a critical examination of any Black emotion will reveal that Black emotions have significantly shaped history and have informed Black agency, Black resistance, and Black people's pursuit for equality in both the past and the present.[23]

Contextualizing the Study

In our study, we examined two recently published Black history textbooks that were created by Black History 365, a new "comprehensive K–12 curriculum company designed for schools across America that takes students and educators on a colorful journey to embracing an inclusive account of American History."[24] Black History 365 was founded by Dr. Walter Milton Jr., a Black, former high school teacher who now serves as CEO of the company. Reflecting on how his fourth-grade teacher erroneously conveyed that African American history commenced with enslavement, Milton—along with Dr. Joel Freeman, a white antiquarian who founded and curated the Freeman Institute Black History Collection—coauthored the Black History 365 textbooks. Adopted in over two hundred school districts across the United States, this textbook collection aims to support the unlearning of historical biases around Black historical narratives and to provide instructors with resources on how to teach Black history in ways that acknowledge Black Americans' contributions and the challenges they have faced.[25] The Black History 365 textbook collection includes three elementary textbooks for third-, fourth-, and fifth-grade classrooms; three middle school textbooks; and a large high school textbook. For this study, we examined the fourth- and fifth-grade elementary textbooks from the series (see table 4.1).

TABLE 4.1 Descriptions of the fourth- and fifth-grade Black History 365 textbooks

Fourth Grade: African Americans Shaping a Nation	*Fifth Grade: African Americans' Contributions to the Arts*
Chapter 1: The Beginning: African Exploration and Founding of America	Chapter 1: African American Arts in Early America: 17th century- 1830
Chapter 2: African Americans in the New Country	Chapter 2: African American Art and Culture during the Antebellum period: 1783–1861
Chapter 3: African Americans Fight for Freedom	Chapter 3: African American church: Influence on the Arts and Culture
Chapter 4: The African-American Story: Emancipation and Freedom	Chapter 4: The Harlem Renaissance 1920s–1930s
	Chapter 5: Black is Beautiful African American culture and identity in the 60s and 70s
	Chapter 6: African American Art and Culture: From Post World War II to Doo-Wop to Modern Hip Hop

We conducted a literary analysis of the fourth- and fifth-grade Black History 365 elementary textbooks to examine how the authors discussed Black rage and/or emotions and feelings akin to Black rage (e.g., anger).[26] The following research questions guided our analysis:

- Which emotions are present in the fourth- and fifth-grade Black History 365 textbooks?
- How is rage, or emotions and feelings akin to rage, depicted and/or described when discussing how African Americans shaped the nation in the fourth-grade textbook?
- How is rage, or emotions and feelings akin to rage, depicted and/or described when discussing African Americans' contributions to the arts in the fifth-grade textbook?

Our literary analysis of the fourth- and fifth-grade Black History 365 textbooks produced two findings. Our first finding illuminated how emotions and feelings associated with rage are absent when describing how Black Americans shaped the nation. Our second finding revealed that the textbook authors omitted any references to Black rage when describing Black people's motivations for creating art. Throughout our findings section, we use language offered by psychologists that positions emotions and feelings into "negative" or "positive" binaries to differentiate between the types of emotions and feelings we found in our analysis.[27] For example, we label emotions and feelings related to joy as "positive emotions/feelings," and emotions and feelings related to rage we label as "negative emotions." We acknowledge that labeling emotions and feelings as "negative" or "positive" produces subjective binaries that oversimplify the emotions that people feel and want to make clear that we use this labeling mechanism for clarity purposes only.

TEACHING BLACK HISTORIES WITHOUT FEELING RAGE

Teaching How Black Americans Shaped the Nation Without Rage

In our analysis of the fourth-grade textbook, we found that the authors omitted references to rage when describing how African Americans shaped the nation. The omission of rage is ironic in this context, given the multiple references that the authors make to Black suffering, Black resistance, and the "notable achievements of Black people" throughout the textbook. When discussing the cruelty of enslavement, the authors wrote:

> Enslaved people worked in the tobacco fields, cotton fields, and vegetable fields in the Southern colonies. Many times, they were beaten and whipped by the plantation overseers. They worked long hours and had very little rest during the workday. Other enslaved African Americans worked inside the plantation homes as house servants, nannies, laundresses, and cooks. Whether they were treated nicely by their owners or not, enslavement was an awful way of living.[28]

Although this passage is not historically inaccurate, as it is true that enslaved African Americans were tortured and subjected to forced labor, this passage fails to acknowledge any Black emotionality. The authors noted that Black people were beaten and whipped, but they fail to describe how enduring beatings and whippings made Black people feel. The authors contended that enslaved people worked long days without rest and claimed that enslavement was awful but failed to explicitly name how the horrors of enslavement made Black people feel. Only describing the cruelty of enslavement and omitting how enslavement made Black people feel can diminish opportunities for elementary students to strengthen their understanding and their historical empathy around enslavement.

Throughout the fourth-grade text, the authors also had sections where they discussed "notable African Americans," whom they described as freedom seekers, abolitionists, war heroes, or activists. However, in their descriptions of these people, the authors failed to use any negative emotions and feelings to describe the "notable African Americans." For example, the authors described Harriet Tubman as "intelligent, rugged and courageous"; Crispus Attucks was described as "a brave martyr"; Robert Smalls was "an enslaved Black American [who] accomplished a daring, seemingly impossible feat"; and Octavius Catto was "a scholar, educator, activist, and renaissance man."[29] While the authors used language that would be associated with producing positive feelings (e.g., Tubman's courage) to describe these people, we ask, "Where is the rage?" The absence of emotions and feelings related to rage is glaring because the very reasons that these people are being described as "notable" are due to their acts of resistance against systems that would likely also produce emotions and feelings synonymous with rage. Indeed, there are plenty of historical sources that explicitly illustrate Harriet Tubman's rage toward enslavement.

Teaching About Black Americans' Contributions to Arts Without Rage

Our analysis of the fifth-grade textbook revealed that emotions played a significant factor in why Black people created art; however, the emotions and feelings that the authors cited to explain why Black people created art were limited to only positive emotions and feelings, while any emotions and feelings related to negative emotions and feelings, particularly rage or aggression, were omitted from the textbook. Similar to the first finding, the omission of rage, or emotions and feelings synonymous with rage, is ironic because the authors make claims that Black people created art as a response to the multiple ways they experienced suffering. For example, in the Preface of the textbook, the authors stated that "The African American story is one of *survival* and *perseverance*," and in the first paragraph of chapter 1, the authors noted: "The first known African American writers were inspired to write about their *tough* times in colonial America. African American writers shared stories about how *enslaved people were treated*. They wrote books about the *unjust treatment* of Black people and their fight for freedom and dignity."[30]

While the authors made claims that early Black writers were motivated by "tough times" or "unjust treatments," the emotions and feelings that the authors used throughout the textbook to describe Black writers' motivations do not reflect all the emotions and feelings produced from experiencing unjust treatment. When describing why enslaved Black people wrote poems and stories, the authors stated, "Literature was a means to confront the cruelty that enslaved people endured. . . . They shared the experiences of a people who were captured and enslaved, and yet survived."[31] The writers put Black people's *hopes* and *grievances* into words. In this example, the authors contended that writing was a way to confront the cruelty that Black people experienced, but two sentences later, they wrote that Black people's feelings of hope and grievances inspired them to put words into paper. While experiencing cruelty can certainly cause one to feel grievance, experiencing cruelty can also produce emotions and feelings such as anger, resentment, or frustration.

Similarly, in chapter 6, which focuses on African American art post–World War II, the authors introduced James Baldwin, noting that his work both "spoke to the pain and struggle of African Americans" as well as examined "the racial tensions in America."[32] The authors concluded Baldwin's section by stating that his writings were "eloquent with an honesty that made his books all best sellers."[33] To teach about Baldwin and his influential writings without naming or even mentioning any emotions or feelings related to rage diminishes the significance of Baldwin's work and misrepresents who he was. One of Baldwin's most famous quotes, which also serves as a central theme in much of his work, exemplifies how Black rage functions as a form of Black consciousness.[34] This awareness not only encompasses Black people's understanding of their existence in an anti-Black world but also speaks to Black people's awareness of the permanence of anti-Blackness that exists within society. While the authors evaded Baldwin's rage, they explicitly characterized his work as "eloquent honesty" and attributed this eloquence to the success of his books. This narrative implies that Baldwin's work resonated with audiences solely because he eloquently addressed the challenges of Black life. However, it was Baldwin's rage that rendered his books compelling, and it is the source of his ongoing inspiration for people today.

Shifting away from a literary focus, chapters 3, 4, and 5 delve into the African American church, the Harlem Renaissance, and African American culture in the sixties, respectively. Within these chapters, the authors explore how the emotions and feelings produced from experiencing oppression motivated Black artists to craft songs, create paintings, and develop scripts for Black television shows. Like the chapters on literature, however, the authors fail to explicitly name any negative emotions when describing Black artists' motivations. For example, the authors stated that Negro Spirituals served as a constant "reminder of the suffering of enslaved African Americans and the belief that suffering would end."[35] They also maintained that Negro Spirituals blended notions of "hope and strength."[36] While Negro Spirituals do convey emotions and feelings of hope and strength, they were also created to remember Black suffering and do convey emotions of rage, grief, and even bitterness.[37] Negro spirituals are important to Black history because they are musical expressions of Black humanity that illuminate the *full range* of Black emotions and feelings.

The findings from our analysis of the fourth- and fifth-grade textbooks are important ideas that educators should grapple with when deciding how they are going to use textbooks to teach Black history in their classrooms. Black rage, and the feelings that it produces, is an emotion that Black people experience when they *feel* their Blackness in an anti-Black society. This feeling of Black rage does not produce anger but rather acts as an impetus for Black people to resist anti-Blackness. To teach children about how and why Black people shaped a nation or how Black people created art without mentioning rage diminishes how rage, oftentimes, operated as a form of resistance. Naming positive emotions does not invalidate the information provided in the textbooks, nor is it inaccurate Black history. Naming only positive emotions, however, when teaching Black histories distorts, oversimplifies, and misrepresents the nuances of Black history education, and it reduces Black humanity and Black identities to Black caricatures who can only be happy and feel joy.

IMPLICATIONS FOR PRACTICE

Findings from our study highlight the need for curriculum materials to attend to the full range of emotions that Black people have experienced throughout history. However, when curriculum materials depict Black bodies as constantly experiencing suffering yet only use positive emotions and feelings, such as joy or hope, to describe Black people's perseverance, strength, or determination, we are left wondering:

- How are students' understandings of Black histories distorted or incomplete when Black people are not portrayed as feeling rage or anger, despite experiencing suffering?
- What messages are students and teachers receiving about the emotions and feelings that Black people are supposed to feel and express in both the past and the present?
- How might textbooks or other curriculum materials that depict Black suffering without acknowledging Black people's feelings of rage or anger impact Black students' perceptions of the emotions they are *allowed* to feel and express in the present?

These are important questions for educators to consider when deciding how to use textbooks and other resources to teach Black histories in ways that highlight how Black people's emotions have acted as catalysts for resistance against anti-Blackness. In the following section, we offer a pedagogical framework known as CARE, which you can use to effectively incorporate emotions into your instruction on Black history.[38]

Critical Analysis of Racialized Emotions (CARE)

Jones's critical analysis of racialized emotions, CARE, is a humanizing and antiracist framework that incorporates theories of racialized emotions and Transformative Social and Emotional Learning, which you can use to guide students through a critical analysis of emotions within historical sources.[39] This framework has the potential to strengthen students' historical thinking skills and also foster students' historical empathy, as this strategy provides opportunities for students to reflect on people's feelings and emotions in the past through a racialized lens. Even more, CARE is not a pedagogical strategy specific to Black history instruction but rather should be used to examine racialized emotions within historical sources broadly—especially when engaging in a critical interrogation of whiteness and white supremacy throughout history. Last, CARE is guided by five questions that can be used with a plethora of historical sources across a variety of modalities ranging from written documents to images, songs, and so on.

As we discussed earlier in this chapter, we acknowledge that some teachers, especially white teachers, might be hesitant to discuss Black rage with their students for fear of reproducing harmful stereotypes about Black people. Although this fear may produce discomfort for teachers, we believe that incorporating Black people's feelings of rage and anger as part of Black history education is necessary to teach Black histories effectively; thus, we offer cautions educators should consider when using this framework. Additionally, we acknowledge that some educators do not embody antiracist beliefs within their personal lives and, subsequently, do not use antiracist pedagogies in their classrooms. Because CARE is a framework steeped in antiracist concepts, we recognize that these educators likely won't use CARE in their classrooms.

Below we apply the five questions from the CARE framework to an activity offered in the fifth-grade Black History 365 textbook, where students were instructed to "Pause and Reflect"[40] on the lyrics below from James Brown's "Say It Loud, I'm Black and I'm Proud."[41] After each CARE question, we discuss its utility within the CARE strategy and provide a sample response on how a student might answer the question.

> Some people say we got a lot of malice
> Some say it's a lotta nerve
> But I say we won't quit movin'

Until we get what we deserve . . .
Say it loud—I'm Black and I'm proud!

CARE QUESTION 1: *What emotions/feelings are present in the source?* This question is designed to have students analyze the emotions and feelings found in the source. If using the source above, some emotions or feelings students may indicate are "malice" and "pride."

CAUTION: Ensure that there are established classroom norms that cultivate an equitable and respectful learning environment, which all participants are aware of and have agreed to uphold.

CARE QUESTION 2: *Whose emotions/feelings are being described or referenced in the source?* This question requires you to provide contextual knowledge about the source or subject. Using the example above, students might indicate that the source is describing James Brown's feelings, or they might infer that the "we" referenced in the song is other Black people and note that Black people's emotions/feelings are being described.

CAUTION: Avoid positioning Students of Color as emotional experts of the racialized people with which they identify.

CARE QUESTION 3: *How do emotions/feelings intersect with race, power, oppression, and/or resistance in the source?* This question is designed to have students examine cause and effect by asking students to analyze what may have caused the historical figures to experience or write about the emotions or feelings expressed in the source. Like Question 2, for students to effectively engage with this question, you need to explain to students what it means to feel race in a racialized society. To do so, you might provide students with contextual knowledge about the events that were happening around the time this source was published or released. Using the example above, you might tell your students that this song was released four months after the assassination of Rev. Dr. Martin Luther King Jr. Having this knowledge, students might respond to this question by making connections between being Black and feeling malice (toward King's assassination), and how that feeling of malice inspired Black people to not quit" and keep "movin'," or to keep engaging in resistance against anti-Blackness.

CAUTION: Be sure that you and your students have a working understanding of race, power, oppression, and resistance.

CARE QUESTION 4: *Do you think that people feel race today in the same ways that people's feelings of race are described in the source? If so, how? If not, why?* This question is designed to have students examine continuity and change by asking students to consider how emotions intersect with race, power, oppression, and/or resistance in the present. Before asking students to answer this question, you should remind students what it means to *feel race* in society. A possible student response may be: Yes, I remember watching the murder of George Floyd and feeling angry, so I participated in a protest that happened in my neighborhood as an act of resistance.

CAUTION: Avoid asking students to put themselves in the "emotional shoes" of historical figures.

CARE QUESTION 5: *What connections can be made about the ways race and emotions/feelings impacted people's actions throughout history? How do your emotions/feelings of race impact how you understand history? How do your emotions/feelings of race impact your actions, interactions, and reactions to injustices in the world?* This question compels students to consider the role that racialized emotions have in history, and it creates opportunities for students to reflect on how their racialized emotions inform their understandings of history. Additionally, this question pushes students to consider how their racialized emotions impact their experiences with and to injustices within society,

CAUTION: Communicate to your students that they are not obligated to share their answers and that feeling apathy is an important emotion. Explain to your students that an analysis of their racialized emotions should not be used to justify hate, white supremacy, and/or anti-Blackness.

The CARE framework seeks to move beyond the uncritical and cognitively focused approaches typically found in social studies education. As Maribel Santiago and Tadashi Dozono have asserted, historical inquiry is too often understood and enacted in classrooms "solely as a cognitive exercise [which] obscures its embedded criticality."[42] As a critical historical inquiry framework, CARE goes beyond asking students to use historical sources to examine cause and effect or continuity and change. Instead, CARE asks students to analyze how the intersection of race, emotion, and power within historical sources inform cause and effect and continuity and change throughout history. CARE also addresses the problem Dozono raised about how historical thinking risks denying students, particularly Students of Color, opportunities to make sense of their own racialized experiences by asking students to consider how their emotions and feelings of race impact how they understand history and their (inter)actions within the world.[43] This approach offers students opportunities to "confront and historicize their experiences in a racialized world."[44]

CARE also provides a unique contribution to the ways students and educators engage with historical empathy, which focuses on "how people from the past thought, felt, made decisions, acted, and faced consequences within a specific historical and social context."[45] Jason Endacott and Sarah Brooks identified three interrelated concepts that comprise historical empathy: historical contextualization, perspective taking, and affective connection. Missing from these concepts, however, is criticality. Why do we ask students to investigate historical contexts, take perspectives, and consider historical figures' affective responses if we are not asking students how these concepts explicitly relate to race, power, oppression, and/or resistance? Even more, what is the purpose of asking students to engage in historical empathy if they do not use what they learn to engage in an empathetic critique of the present and work toward a more socially just future? CARE cultivates space for students to do both. First, CARE asks students to interrogate how race informs people's feelings and their decision-making, historically and contemporarily. Second, CARE invites students to investigate how their racialized feelings impact their actions, interactions, and reactions to injustices in the present.

CLOSING THOUGHTS

In this chapter, we discussed findings from our study, which illustrated how a Black history textbook tended to depict Black people as only feeling Black joy or other positive emotions despite experiencing constant suffering. We argue that when textbooks and other curriculum materials focus solely on Black people's joy, they create oversimplified portrayals of Black historical narratives that dehumanize Black people and erase Black agency. We invite educators to use the CARE framework in their instruction to present more nuanced narratives of Black experiences—narratives that both acknowledge how Black people's emotions impact their historical and contemporary struggles against anti-Blackness and that honor the complexity of Black life and resilience.

As former K–12 educators and scholars of Black history education, we find value in centering *all* Black emotions and feelings when teaching Black histories.

Integrating analysis of Black emotions into Black history education is not just an additive approach but a transformative one. We believe that such an approach does more than educate; it humanizes, empowers, and inspires students to engage with history in a way that is both reflective and active, cultivating a generation that is more informed, critically empathetic, and equipped to challenge injustices. This is the future of Black history education—one that fully embraces the intellectual, emotional, and agentive nature of Black humanity.

CHAPTER 5

"Remediando" Latinx Blackness: AfroIndigenous Spiritual Practice as History Pedagogy

ELIANA CASTRO AND KRISTA L. CORTES

For better or for worse, students experience identity formation as much through the formal learning that takes place in schools as the informal learning that occurs elsewhere. In the United States, this reality presents a challenge for students who identify as Black, Indigenous, Latinx, Asian American, or Pacific Islander.[1] An abundance of research has shown that Black children miss out on childhood due to the theft of their racial innocence.[2] Latinx children, too, are consistently confronted from an early age with how they are racialized. This problem is, therefore, compounded for people who identify as both Black *and* Latinx.

Though schools are microcosms of the anti-Black, racist, nativist, xenophobic, sexist, heteronormative, settler-colonial, and otherwise oppressive world in which we live, there are ways to transform racially minoritized students' schooling experiences into joyful and affirming processes that elevate them and their communities. This goal is especially elusive for students at the intersections of various marginalized identities, but it is not impossible.

History education about AfroLatinx identities and experiences presents a site of potential resistance to Eurocentric ways of teaching and learning. Educational spaces compel AfroLatinx students to attend to the intersections of their Blackness and Latinidad with a multitude of fluid factors—migration status, language, colorism, geographical location, and other dynamic facets of their existence—often without support. This chapter reorients history pedagogy by offering Afro-Indigenous spiritual practices as a type and means of knowledge formation.[3] We use a sociocultural lens to offer ideas for designing learning environments and experiences that are attuned to the sociohistorical and contemporary specificities of some AfroLatinx student experiences. This approach, rooted in African knowledges, rests on liberatory practices developed, implemented, and passed down by generations of Afrodiasporic peoples who were, and continue to be, marginalized by society. Enacting this form of reclamation and resistance is both a consequence of and an avenue to (re)center students' racialized experiences within the educational paradigms that dominate US schools. It is also, we argue, a healing practice.

As AfroLatinx scholars, we seek to introduce K–12 educators and researchers to a model for teaching through, with, and about AfroIndigenous spiritual practices. This approach defies Eurodominant conceptions of knowledge, exposes un(der)told Afrodiasporic histories, interrogates contemporary AfroLatinx identities and experiences, and promotes the visioning of possible AfroLatinx futures. We begin by making a case for why we focus on AfroLatinx youth and explaining how we conceive of Blackness and Latinidad. Next, we provide historical context for how AfroIndigenous spiritual practices took on personal and political importance for many Afrodiasporic peoples. The third section develops the concept of AfroIndigenous spiritual practice as knowledge formation to make the case for how we bind the notions of remediation and the Spanish verb remediar to form "remediando" in history pedagogy. We then introduce syncretic (blended or combined) learning and remediation as praxis that blurs the differences between everyday and school-based knowledges, promoting alignment of learners' interests and academic goals. Building from this, we draw parallels between the syncretic faith practices of our ancestors and the application of those principles in history education. This approach constitutes what we refer to as "remediando," or healing, as a model of teaching and learning that emulates key features of AfroIndigenous spiritual practices. To close, we illustrate how these strategies may look in a K–12 classroom, including how they may relate to content standards or curriculum frameworks, and we offer some resources for educators to consider.

Our pedagogical suggestions include strategies for the creation of spaces, activities, and roles that highlight everyday resistance in the AfroIndigenous tradition.

The chapter is intended for educators and scholars who are working and learning alongside AfroLatinx children and youth. The concepts developed and strategies proposed here may not be universal across all Latinx-origin communities of African descent, nor should individuals adopt them if they have no connection or commitment to AfroLatinx students. They are student-centered interventions for engaging with the past and must be undertaken with emancipatory and liberatory aims at heart. Lastly, we acknowledge that educators may face challenges regarding the "legitimacy" of these topics and approaches, and we respond by exploring potential benefits to K–12 teachers and students who engage with this paradigm.

WHY AFROLATINX STUDENTS?

The authors see it fit to foreground their identities as unhyphenated AfroLatinas with Caribbean roots. The first author (Eliana Castro) is Dominican born, the granddaughter of a syncretic spiritist, herbalist, and devout Catholic. Her personal experiences as a first-generation AfroLatina migrant and mother, her professional background as a former urban high school history/social studies teacher, and her current role as a secondary history/social studies teacher educator all inform her perspectives. The second author (Krista L. Cortes) is a self-identified AfroPuerto Rican, born and raised in the diaspora, whose early years were spent in New York but has since made home in multiple locales. Cortes brings to this offering her perspectives as a practicing Santera, the mother of AfroLatinx children, and someone who has worked for social change as an educator in K–16 settings for over a decade. We enter this work mindful of the immeasurable scope of variability among Afrodiasporic—and specifically AfroLatinx—communities. Broadly, we do not essentialize Blackness, Latinidad, or AfroLatinidad. For instance, we push back on common misconceptions of AfroLatinxs as geographically confined to the Hispanophone Latin American tropics, specifically the Caribbean islands. There are distinct and unique AfroLatinx communities everywhere, from Alaska to Tierra del Fuego.

As AfroLatinas, mothers, and educators, we recognize the urgency to celebrate youth who exist at the intersections of Blackness and Latinidad, as well as how classroom practices and policies reflect their lived experiences back to them. We see a need to understand how AfroLatinx youth make sense of who they are in relation to their multiracial and multiethnic communities and how these shifting identities are impacted by classroom practices.

We unequivocally set out to reclaim Blackness as a *cultural practice* that is deeply embedded in Latinidad for the millions of AfroLatinx people living in the United States, including those in K–12. AfroIndigenous is a term we have adapted to reflect the ways Blackness has become native to people, places, and practices throughout Latin America and the Caribbean. That is to say, AfroIndigeneity represents identities "richly embedded with cultural meaning and socio-historical context that today inform subaltern subjectivity . . . [and] resist dominant ideological constructions."[4] Our conception of AfroLatinidades aligns with Augustin Lao Montes's attention to the "overlapping diasporas" that create multiple ways of doing, being, and imagining AfroLatinidad.[5] To be AfroIndigenous is to carry complex and layered histories and political processes that are still unfolding to this day. Far from a static or one-dimensional existence, it is one that is at once rich with beauty and rife with conflict; we hold this complexity as a strength.

CONTEXT

Since the inception of humanity's largest human trafficking operation for the purposes of chattel slavery, the African individuals who survived the grueling transatlantic voyage have landed on "other" shores. Though their bodies were battered and bruised, their spirits were not entirely broken. The diasporas that emerged from the dispersal of African individuals held in bondage attest to the tenacity of the enslaved; those who arrived on lands foreign to them sought out faces, languages, customs, or anything else they might recognize. Despite their abject dehumanization, these too-many millions of enslaved people did the most inherently human thing: they fought tooth and nail to survive, be whole, and live free. Even when existing in relative isolation or not finding a shared past with those in their vicinity, the earliest Africans in Abya Yala, "the Americas," devised ingenious systems for preserving everything from which they had been forcibly separated.[6] This never-ending quest to hold onto what remained of their former homes—to reassemble whole selves—resulted in the clandestine practices of spiritual rituals and ceremonies, native language(s) use, music making, song and dance, herbalism, and other timeless, quotidian expressions of being and knowing. By cleaving to what European enslavers attempted to strip from them, our enslaved African ancestors fashioned uniquely resilient ways of being. Today, many of us return to those traditions to heal our present wounds and extend the tenacious tendrils of the past into the future.

One community that was able to safeguard the African spiritual practices they inherited, even as they forged new instantiations of them in a new place, was the maroons. Maroons, or cimarrones in Spanish, were enslaved people who successfully fled the plantation system and enjoyed a tentative fugitive freedom.[7] Maroons could be individuals who operated in isolation or as members of collectives. Their flight was often meticulously premeditated but also sometimes spontaneous. Whether alone or in concert, the manifestation of forethought or impulse, marronage was the utter refusal of—though not altogether a retreat from—the institution of slavery and the society born of it. Maroon communities, variably known as manieles, quilombos, and palenques throughout different parts of Latin America, were known to carry out guerilla offensives selectively; they poisoned water sources, stole food and supplies, and are believed to have even intervened in armed conflicts between European colonial powers—most notably, Sir Francis Drake vanquishing the Spanish.[8]

More often than not, though, the continued practice of spirituality required subversive and adaptive means. While some African individuals in the Americas were able to practice their faith unabated, unabridged, and unadulterated, many more were obligated by their circumstances to forge a new way of moving in and out of their spiritual realms. One strategy to evade notice was syncretism. Syncretic spiritual practice was a strategic commingling of that which Western societies have simplistically dichotomized as sacred and profane. AfroIndigenous syncretism is more than that. Even beyond the first generation after landing on this continent, Afrodescended faith practitioners retained elements of their belief systems that were integral to their views on living and dying, especially if those components were compatible with Christian modes of worship. Two such examples are the veneration of the cross and the reverence of a trinity, both of which predated contact with Europeans in several African cultures.[9] This tactical tolerance was fundamental. By embracing and customizing Christian ideals, Africans in the Americas ensured that their traditions would endure under the guise of conversion and devotion to the colonial faith, typically Catholicism. African spirituality was transformed, with elements of Christianity superimposed on, but not overpowering it. In this way, syncretism bears witness to how our African ancestors subverted spiritual supremacy to survive without losing themselves.

APPROACH TO THE PAST: AFROINDIGENOUS SPIRITUAL PRACTICES AS KNOWLEDGE FORMATION

Everyday spirituality enables AfroLatinx communities to make meaning and develop a sense of belonging; therefore, history pedagogy that aligns with these practices can reflect and affirm AfroLatinidad.[10] Against the historical backdrop of how Afrodescendants in what is now known as Latin America reinvented their African spiritualities, AfroLatinidad is imbued with meaning that is shaped by these sociohistorical shifts. AfroLatinx spiritualities depend on, normalize, and actively elevate knowledge that is inherited and passed on through shared practices. Moreover, AfroIndigenous spiritual practices forge new forms of knowledge as they continue to morph to meet the needs of each space and time.

One way believers seek to be enlightened with knowledges and perspectives about the past, present, and future is by consulting with those who have transcended into the ancestral realm. Closely related to this ancestor worship is the folk interpretation of dreams. AfroIndigenous spiritual practitioners believe that, through dreams, "the desires of the spirits are communicated to the living";[11] dreams create opportunities to connect with our spiritual lineage. Because cultural practices like the interpretation of dreams can persist across borders and generations, they become displays of diaspora. Interrogating dreams can, therefore, be a form of everyday spirituality from which some AfroLatinx communities draw to make meaning and develop a sense of belonging.

Many AfroLatinxs carry with/in them some form of AfroIndigenous religion or spirituality—sometimes referred to colloquially as brujería.[12] The term brujería conjures up images of votive candles, spiritual baths, offerings, saints, and santos, becoming an outlet for the expression of spirituality that encompasses myriad ways of living and enacting AfroLatinx Blackness. In their work with Santería practitioners, Helen Rose Ebaugh and Mary Curry found that religious practices, such as storytelling and sacred rituals, created avenues through which ethnic identity was transferred to younger community members.[13] This example highlights how religion and/or spirituality is a mechanism through which practices and identities gain meaning. Despite the differing manifestations of AfroIndigenous spiritualities, it is a facet of AfroLatinx identity that has received little attention in educational contexts, many of which are dominated by Eurocentric paradigms.[14] Therefore, an approach to teaching and learning history that is rooted in AfroLatinx everyday spiritual practices can both reflect and affirm Afro-Latinidad beyond what cognitive frameworks like historical thinking aim to do.[15]

Spiritual practices derived from syncretic African traditions allow AfroLatinx adherents to claim spaces of their own for a doing and being of Blackness and Latinidad that embraces their transgressive AfroLatinx identity.[16] Espiritismo, Santería, Palo, and other AfroIndigenous spiritual practices have played important roles in AfroLatinx resistance to the dehumanizing and oppressive forces operating in and against their communities.[17] These practices, originally promoted and protected by enslaved Africans in Latin America, pushed against colonial-era European domination and provided tools for liberation.[18] They can do so once again.

When students investigate how AfroIndigenous spiritual practices have been vilified and criminalized in Latin America, the Caribbean, the United States, and elsewhere, they can comprehend the grave danger that their enslaved forebears risked to preserve and pass them along. This understanding may help young AfroLatinxs appreciate the significance of these spiritual practices and the empowerment potential they carry. Those who identify with these past and present communities of practice may reevaluate their own notions of what constitutes knowledge and how the "legitimacy" of history has been gatekept by narrow Eurocentric definitions of understanding. Close study of historical and contemporary examples of spiritual ways of knowing, including the role of dreams, could be eye-opening. Students who engage in this type of learning can see themselves and their communities in a new light. They can then "dream" possible pasts and futures that affirm their identities and perspectives.

Aside from the impact this learning can have on AfroLatinx students, teachers can employ this approach as an entry into conversations about epistemology, the study of knowledge and theories about what distinguishes established, justified claims from opinion. Historical thinking importantly encourages students to interrogate the sources of information they use, conduct close readings of texts, interpret information, analyze how context influences content, and corroborate historical claims. However, a history pedagogy that centers AfroLatinx students must also be introspective and conscious of the relationship that students have with the past, the learning of the past, and the open wounds that the process can help or hurt. Borrowing from how AfroIndigenous spiritualities privilege inherited knowledges, teachers can allow ways of being and knowing that are typically not recognized by Eurocentric schooling, including those presented in dreams, to have a meaningful place in the classroom. Dreams then become one of several forms of shared societal memory, construction of historical narratives, and/or perspective-taking and can be considered a valuable source of historical meaning-making.

Although teaching students to consider dreams as historical sources may seem anathema, there is conceptual grounding to justify this unorthodox approach to teaching history. For one, we are cognizant that content standards can be considered a barrier or limitation to the teaching of liberatory content and skills, but it need not be so. A critical, somewhat subversive reading of the national history curriculum guidelines in the College, Career, and Civic Life (C3) Framework may help us illustrate. The intended outcomes around historical sources and evidence for students in grades nine through twelve call for interrogating how current perspectives of the past are limited by the historical sources that represent perspectives of the time, detecting limitations in historical evidence and secondary interpretations, critiquing the usefulness and appropriateness of sources, and integrating evidence from multiple sources to form reasoned arguments. The learning targets lend themselves to the task of challenging the hegemony of the written word and physical documents as the primary legitimate source of credible historical evidence. When one takes up healing as the end and spiritual practice as the means, the "standard" *modus operandi* simply will not suffice. Educators committed to taking up everyday AfroIndigenous spiritual practices must also adopt pedagogical strategies that integrate the whole student. Before examining in detail how the practices that we suggest might look in a K–12 classroom, we outline the conceptual orientations that frame how we propose that these interventions take place.

Remediating/"Remediando" History Pedagogy: Promoting Alignment of Learners' Interests and Academic Goals

History education is suffering a crisis of disassociation. It often alienates the past from the full personhood and humanity of those who study it. Reorganizing history pedagogy toward new paradigms that are asset-based and center students' racialized experiences requires a radical imagination that takes seriously both the intersections of multiple identities and the socioemotional well-being of students.[19] History then becomes a potent salve. Classroom spaces have been most responsive to the needs of nondominant students when the inherited and embodied knowledges that these students already have is used to bridge the everyday and complement the academic to enhance both in meaningful and rigorous ways—that is, adopting a syncretic approach.[20] A syncretic approach to teaching and learning suggests that overlaying different ways of knowing and being, especially those that are important and valued by the communities in which we teach, can create points of convergence where learners' interests and academic pursuits can be developed. By shifting our focus to cultural practices and ways of knowing we disrupt deficit frameworks and knowledge hierarchies by creating opportunities for students to engage with ideas and practices that are meaningful.[21]

We previously discussed the ingenuity of AfroLatinx communities who found ways to persist in their practice of AfroIndigenous religions and spirituality while masking it within the dominant and accepted forms of Christianity they were meant to adopt. This syncretism describes "the attempted reconciliation or union of different or opposing principles, practices, or parries, as in philosophy or religion."[22] This same principle of syncretism can describe our aim of bringing together everyday knowledges with target academic conventions in a way that disrupts the privileging of academic knowledge at the expense of inherited knowledges. A syncretic approach intentionally brings together "everyday and formal practices . . . to meet our goal of organizing viable pathways for nondominant communities to participate in and create new forms of action."[23] Much like the insurgent syncretism of our African forebears, AfroLatinx students can stitch together some formal components of so-called academic learning to preserve the practices that sustain them. Educators can facilitate this process through curriculum design and implementation of syncretic learning environments.

In such syncretic learning environments, educators are involved in the process of shaping historical actors, that is, learners who are conscious and intentional designers of their own futures. A historical actor, thus, "involves developing a sense of one's own identity in the broad context of time, including how particular cultural practices came into being and how they have enabled and constrained possibilities for learning, and how these understandings inform future-oriented practices."[24] Becoming a historical actor requires recognizing oneself as historicized and developing the necessary tools to understand one's "experiences as produced through lived history (Holland, Lachicotte, Skinner, & Cain, 1998)."[25] By bringing a syncretic approach into the classroom, teachers can position young AfroLatinxs as historical actors able to transform the present and future in culturally relevant and sustaining ways.[26]

The development of a syncretic learning environment thus requires a holistic reorganization of the learning context—changes can be both physical and intangible. History educators invested in creating learning environments that reflect a nuanced and fluid conception of Blackness can transform the spaces where learning history happens, the tools utilized, the activities carried out, and the roles assumed by teachers and students alike. Working with/in AfroIndigenous knowledge paradigms and using traditional Afrocentric methods of understanding the world, we seek to expand our understanding of remediation.[27]

To do this, we bind the notions of remediation and the Spanish verb "remediar" to form our conception of remediating/"remediando" Latinx Blackness in history education. In Spanish, "remediar" connotes to remedy, set right, or improve. The noun "remedio" implies a means—often homemade—for soothing, curing, or healing. While scholars have written extensively about the sociocultural concept of remediation through the use of cultural tools, our formulation of remediation/remedio emphasizes the centering of Afrodescendants in the process of learning for healing. Therefore, remediating/"remediando" acts on the complementary desires to

- include and foreground histories that are not preserved in the written record;
- disrupt (i.e., remedy) the bifurcation of knowledge into disciplines; and
- harness the healing power of how connecting that which has previously been fragmented can breathe wholeness and wellness into historical wounds.

Many Black and Latinx communities' histories were either never documented in writing, lost to time, hidden, or destroyed. By including and foregrounding them in our history pedagogy, we acknowledge their significance, honor the role of oral and artistic preservation, and recognize the range of experiences that we may never fully know. To remedy the bifurcation of knowledges is to reintegrate components of our humanity that experience their fullest expression when allowed to organically interact with other aspects of our whole selves—the mind, body, and soul.

Lastly, accomplishing the first two objectives allows educators to hold space for students to explore parts of themselves that may have been silenced, erased, and distorted. AfroLatinx youth can thus connect with their learning and heal the hurts of historical wounds.

Taken together, these priorities not only upend the use of "remedial" to connote a classification of academics intended for students framed in deficit perspectives but shift history pedagogy toward a new paradigm altogether. In so doing, educators can develop an ethos for teaching that values and privileges Black knowledges and ways of being. For example, allowing students to relate material to their lived experience, or that of their families, and how historical events have impacted their everyday lives is one way of reorganizing the learning environment. Additionally, creating opportunities for students to assert how they feel and considering this as valid and vital for the understanding of historical content is in line with remediating classroom spaces. That is to say, just as our ancestors preserved their traditional African spirituality by masking it with the appearance of adherence to Christianity, educators can adopt a history pedagogy that, at first glance, simply aligns with content standards but whose main goal is to retain an Afrocentric focus.

"Remediando" history pedagogy extends beyond cognitive historical thinking skills by turning the learner's eye inward and by holding space for embodied experiences, a holistic worldview, and the integration of the self into the broader context of time as a historical actor. This approach aims to fully humanize AfroLatinx youth and enables them to forge a path to their liberation, one where they can see their place in their families, communities, and ancestral lineages across the globe.[28] When young people with marginalized identities can see themselves as wholly human throughout all of history, they may be less likely to pathologize themselves and their communities, moving instead to a stance of aligning their powerful past with an auspicious future. Skills alone do not ground the soul like that.

IMPLICATIONS FOR PRACTICE

As mentioned previously, remediating/"remediando" may require adding "tools" and activities to the learning ecology, redefining the primary roles and how they interact with one another, or physically changing spaces to position Blackness at the core of instructional design. In order to eschew a utilitarian, capitalist framing of these practices as merely functional or extractive, we will refrain from referring to them as tools; we will instead call them media (as in, the plural of "a medium"). This term is consistent with AfroIndigenous spiritual practices based on kinship and community, where people and objects can be vessels and channels for spirits. It also acts as a reminder that this deeply spiritual approach to teaching and learning history is not merely another conventional historical thinking skill. It is profoundly personal and embodied engagement with the past that foregrounds forms of knowing that are typically excluded from formal learning.

While not exhaustive, our suggested strategies illustrate how our proposed approach to remediating/"remediando" might look in a K–12 classroom or other history learning space. As with all skillful instructional design, such remediation/remedio necessitates careful planning, thoughtful organizing, and creative improvising. But unlike most conventional history pedagogy, this syncretic approach brings the entire personhood of teachers and learners into the process of exploring the past to make sense of the present and shape the future. In this vision we are setting forth, history educators—broadly defined to mean anyone who facilitates learning about the past—must step outside the conventional roles of a teacher vis-à-vis students to design AfroLatinx-engaged environments. We offer some ideas of this syncretic praxis below.

Illustrations

In this section, we offer three brief vignettes that depict what syncretic, Afro-Indigenous spiritual practice-oriented history education might look like in a classroom.

- **Uncensoring the Census**: In an activity aimed at challenging the Argentinian self-image as white and European, learners can (1) browse seventeenth-century records of how many enslaved Africans were brought to the River Plate ports in what are now Argentina and Uruguay, (2) analyze Argentine census data on race in the eighteenth century, and (3) discuss how the removal of racial categories from the census allowed authorities to rewrite the national narrative and create a discourse of blanqueamiento. To highlight and counter the experience of erasure that Afrodescendants underwent, members of the learning community would identify an ancestor (fictive or biological kin) whose story they know little about and set out to recover as many fragments as possible of their story from others in their family, community, or other means. They could then write or create a representation of that person's life as a work of speculative historical nonfiction. *Note: Educators should remind students that slavery is but a fraction of the history of African and Afrodescended peoples, but an important one to name in the process of healing historical wounds.*

Some relevant resources include

- *Ancestor Trouble: A Reckoning and a Reconciliation* by Maud Newton
- *Lose Your Mother: A Journey Along the Atlantic Slave Route* by Saidiya Hartman
- The Trans-Atlantic Slave Voyages database (slavevoyages.org)

- **Reading AfroLatinx Literature**: To blur the lines between content areas, students could read memoirs by AfroLatinxs and/or young adult novels to examine the literary devices, the presence of art, and the experiences of spiritual becoming (as well as enduring racism, battling intergenerational differences, witnessing gentrification, and other relatable themes for young adults). To deepen students' engagement with the story of Sierra in Daniel José Older's *Shadowshaper*, for instance, students can create visual art, music, performance, or other expressions of self. The coming-of-age motif common in memoirs and young adult novels lends itself to the creation of rites of passage (also known as age-grade initiations) in the classroom, modeled after rituals and ceremonies in AfroIndigenous spiritual traditions.

  Some relevant resources include

  - *The Altar of My Soul* by Marta Moreno Vega
  - *The Blvd* by Jenise Miller
  - *Daring to Write: Contemporary Narratives by Dominican Women* by Erika Martínez et al.
  - *Daughters of the Stone* by Dahlma Llanos-Figueroa
  - *Down These Mean Streets* by Piri Thomas
  - *The Making of Yolanda La Bruja* by Lorraine Avila
  - *Shadowshaper* by Daniel José Older
  - *Sincerely Sicily* by Tamika Burgess
  - *The Sun and the Void* by Gabriela Romero Lacruz

- **The Kitchen Table**: One way to remediar the classroom space is to imagine new ways of setting up dialogue and engagement with materials. The kitchen table culturally is a space where intergenerational family members discuss important topics, share stories, and engage in food preparation/consumption. This practice is akin to Indigenous peoples' "talking circles," which seek to hold space for listening without judgment and to be in community. Taking inspiration from these many uses, it is possible to create a practice in the classroom that resembles the kitchen table. This may require physically creating a kitchen table with tables and desks available in the classroom or designating a space in the classroom where students and educators can come together to discuss and share. In this space, the sharing of experiences, wonderings, and feelings would be prioritized to understand how students are making sense of classroom content. We suggest collectively setting expectations for the space so that students feel compelled to participate holistically.

  Some relevant resources include

  - *Family Lore* by Elizabeth Acevedo
  - *Kitchen Table Remedios* by Selina Morales https://borderlore.org/kitchen-table-remedios/
  - *Daughter of the Sea* (https://www.youtube.com/watch?v=143xfwKW6Rs)
  - *Kitchen Table Series* by Carrie Weems (https://www.nga.gov/collection/art-object-page.209288.html)
  - *From Past to Present: The Healing Power of Talking Circles* by Trini Tlazohtetl Rodriguez
- **An Altar Orientation**: Across many cultures, altars have been created and used as sites of prayer and ritual. These sacred spaces become physical manifestations of memory and portals that transcend time and space. Building on the work of Norell Martinez, an altar orientation in the classroom can aid educators in nourishing students' bodymindspirits while raising their consciousness and agency. An altar orientation requires that educators are both reflective and reflexive in their praxis; we understand the learning/unlearning we need to do individually to be better teachers for our students and better members of our communities. We offer our students the work that it takes to decolonize our own minds so they, in turn, feel

supported and encouraged to do the same work themselves. An altar orientation also entails naming the silences and gaps in our knowledge, recognizing what stories are not being told and what voices may be missing, and then collectively building out the archive in order to start filling those gaps. Finally, an altar orientation requires sacrificing that which no longer serves us. This means being honest about the violence non-dominant communities have endured but not letting that be the end of our stories.

Some relevant resources include

- *The Altar of My Soul: The Living Traditions of Santería* by Marta Moreno Vega
- *Chicana Art: The Politics of Spiritual and Aesthetic Altarities* by Laura E. Pérez
- "For Sarah Baartman" (song) by Nitty Scott
- *Medicine Stories: Essays for Radicals* by Aurora Levins Morales (includes chapter "The Historian as Curandera" by Aurora Levins Morales)
- *Voices from the Ancestors: Xicanx and Latinx Spiritual Expressions and Healing Practices* by Lara Medina & Martha R. Gonzales (includes chapter "A Pedagogy of Ofrendas: The Altar as a Tool for Integrating Social Justice in the Classroom" by Norell Martínez)

Practical Considerations

We see all of this as rooted in a critical transnational feminist praxis that seeks liberation and decolonization in the Latinx and Black communities by creating new forms of knowing and being.[29] Our work as history educators demands that we attend to the various absences and omissions inherent in how history is told and find ways to address it. This is of particular importance as it pertains to obscured "subjectivities, epistemologies, and lived experiences" such as that of AfroLatinx peoples. This is a feminist project.[30] This does not simply mean "adding back" select figures every now and then in order to increase representation; there must be intentionality and thoughtfulness animating this work.

Our proposed feminist approach is an extension of the orientation known as engaged pedagogy, which emphasizes teaching that respects and cares for students holistically.[31] Engaged pedagogy prioritizes getting to know students deeply, making connections to their families, and fueling their passions to have students make meaningful connections to course content. This type of learning environment requires mutual vulnerability where the teacher begins by acquiescing their power, showing a willingness to get personal, and inviting students to do so as well. These moves resist official Eurocentric knowledge and the Eurocentric roles and relationships that tend to govern the education systems in the United States. By encouraging dialogue that feels equally shared, the classroom becomes a site for consequential change.

Modeling for students how a personal, even spiritual, investment can deepen our learning of the past is crucial for establishing a student-centered curriculum and classroom space. While the illustrations above provide some examples of how remediating/"remediando" can look in a classroom, they are merely suggestions. The specific content that is most relevant in each educator's particular context can vary widely. It may be that students take an active interest in a historical actor, event, or phenomenon; have a personal connection to a place; harbor some hesitation about engaging with traditional African spiritual practices due to their own faith, their complex self-concept, or their internal conflict over racial self-identification. These and other realities will undoubtedly factor into how we educators can broach these topics with students.

Lastly, we would be remiss if we did not reiterate that entering into a profound spiritual relationship with learners and facilitating their relationality to the past requires the utmost care. For many young people, all manner of traumas may have ensconced themselves in their bodies and the bodies of their loved ones, both present and departed. Engaging with new histories or with new media, activities, roles, and learning environments can be raw. Some students may shut down and disengage when these wounds are reopened, while for others the pain inflicted can be less visible. Prepare students for the nature of whatever content and form you decide to take up. Structure the space for each individual to feel seen, heard, and valued. Set agreements that create an environment of grace and loving kindness, of trust and honesty. Ground yourself and open your heart and mind for others to teach you from the recesses of their embodied knowledges. Above all, be observant and remain attuned to how your young people are doing all throughout.

CLOSING THOUGHTS

At this point, you have traveled with us through space and time to arrive at this moment. We hope that you marveled, as we both have, at the tenacity of our ancestors, who did everything within their power to survive and thrive. We firmly believe that learning can and should be joyful and sustaining for Black, Indigenous, Latinx, Asian American, and Pacific Islander youth in this country. We feel convinced that history pedagogies that reflect and affirm AfroLatinx students specifically can help them reconceptualize their place in their families, communities, ancestral lineage, and history overall. We offer the guiding principles of everyday AfroIndigenous spiritual practices to accomplish these goals. This pedagogical approach can bring about healing by disrupting Eurocentric approaches to teaching and learning, centering Afrocentric worldviews and their spiritual manifestations, revealing un(der)told stories, and engaging youth in a profound process of self-reclamation through the study of the past. Young people today need to resort to syncretic insurgency to maintain the sacred things within the mundane.

The concept of remediating/"remediando" Latinx Blackness through history pedagogy is far more than historical thinking skills. It is spirit work. By resisting the notion that wisdom about or knowledge of the past exists only in the mind, we create an openness and flexibility that seamlessly integrates individual being and knowing with their ancestral knowledge and existence.

PART THREE

Storytelling as Healing

CHAPTER 6

Embracing Palestinian Oral Histories and Narratives in History Education

MUNA SALEH

> My argument is that history is made by men and women, just as it can also be unmade and rewritten, always with various silences and elisions, always with shapes imposed and disfigurements tolerated.
>
> —Edward Said[1]

When I was in high school, my social studies teacher told me that my family lied to me about our own history.

Growing up as a Palestinian Muslim girl living in amiskwaciy-wâskahikan in Treaty 6 lands, I cannot recall Palestine and Palestinians even being alluded to

I am grateful for the support, advice, and care of many family and friends, including Christine Martineau, Hanadi Shatara, Amber Smith, and Nawar Hamadeh, throughout my work on this chapter. My sincere appreciation to Tadashi Dozono and Maribel Santiago for your insightful suggestions and for your patience and support throughout the process of bringing this important edited collection to life. Finally, I want to acknowledge that this chapter draws on research supported by the Social Sciences and Humanities Research Council (SSHRC).

in school. This is not shocking, considering I was never taught the truth about the historical and ongoing atrocities that enable(d) the settler-colonization of these lands and across Turtle Island. However, one day in my grade twelve social studies class, we focused on the history of "the Arab-Israeli war of 1948" by reading a few paragraphs from our textbook . . . a textbook that referred to us only as "Arabs" and refused to name Palestine or Palestinians as a peoples. I don't remember the exact words I read from the textbook that day, but I recall shaking with indignation at the mangled version of history I was encountering in class. Incredibly shy, I didn't often raise my hand in class, but I felt the need to push back against the stories being narrated that day. I felt that I would be betraying my family, and especially my beloved grandmother Sittee Charifa (Allah yirhama), if I remained silent. Still shaking, I said that, as a Palestinian, I knew the version of history that the textbook was telling was not true. I shared how both sides of my family had been violently dispossessed and displaced from our lands in early May of 1948 during the Nakba.[2] I shared how I grew up in a large intergenerational family home with my grandmother, Sittee Charifa (Allah yerhama), and that Sittee still lived with a bullet lodged in her back because of the violent attack on our village of Mughar Al-Khayt in Palestine by Zionist militia during the Nakba.[3] I don't remember my teacher's exact response to my words that day, but he said something akin to how my family is obviously "biased," that the version of history I was taught at home was inaccurate, and that I should turn to "credible" historical sources to learn the truth behind this "conflict."

In this chapter, I explore how embracing Palestinian oral histories and narratives holds educative and transformative potential for history education. My story of being confronted in class with racist and dehumanizing narratives about Palestinian history is not unique to me or something of a bygone age. Colonial mythologies about Palestinians, Palestine, and Palestinian history, rooted in a long history of colonial and orientalist narratives in/by the West that dehumanize Arabs, Palestinians, and Muslims as violent uncivilized nonperson "others," are ubiquitous and ongoing in social studies and history education.[4] There is an ongoing refusal of Palestinian (oral) histories and narratives—particularly the intergenerational storytelling practices of Palestinian women—as profoundly onto-epistemological and political acts of re/storying what is deemed "legitimate" knowledge and history and as liberatory acts of truth-telling and resistance against silencing and erasure.[5]

Palestinian intergenerational oral transmission of knowledge, history, and memory has defied and powerfully resisted colonial mythologies that "removed the native Palestinian from the unfolding of history, as their presence would cause embarrassment to a celebration of an otherwise successful colonial mission."[6] Ahmed Sa'di described these colonial mythologies—where Palestinians simply disappeared—as "one important strategy of un-narration."[7] Sa'di's words, alongside historical and ongoing Palestinian resistances, bring to mind Edward Said's contention from over forty years ago that Palestinian narratives have not only been nonexistent in Western media and discourses, Zionist narratives about Palestine and Palestinians have been dominant.[8] Said argued that "permission to narrate" is ultimately about who has the power to narrate a people's story.[9] Said asserted, "Now the Palestinians are only abstractions in remarks made about them. Tomorrow they will become actualities, not because they were not in fact actualities before, but because the West must concede that history is more than Western history."[10]

Not only is history more than Western history, but history is more than written documentation or archived material. For Palestine and Palestinians, oral traditions and histories have been vital to narrating ourselves and our history and resisting colonial mythologies and erasure. As Nur Masalha stressed, "Narrative histories, memory and oral history have become a key genre of Palestinian historiography—a sub-discipline whose function is to guard against the 'disappearance from history' of the Palestinian people."[11] Linda Tuhiwai Smith (Ngāti Awa, Ngāti Porou, Tūhourangi) argued that even the term "oral traditions" can be misleading as this involves more than simply telling stories or teaching traditions, but reclaiming the past alongside bearing witness, giving testimony, restoring the spirit, and demanding justice.[12] Smith asserted,

> Telling our stories from the past, reclaiming the past, giving testimony to the injustices of the past are all strategies which are commonly employed by Indigenous peoples struggling for justice. On the international scene, it is extremely rare and unusual when Indigenous accounts are accepted and acknowledged as valid interpretations of what has taken place. And yet, the need to tell our stories remains the powerful imperative of a powerful form of resistance.[13]

Rosemary Sayigh contended that although global Indigenous peoples have orally disseminated knowledge and histories for centuries, only more recently have historians in the West acknowledged these onto-epistemologies as a way of better understanding historical and ongoing events, systems, and processes.[14] Particularly relevant for history education, Sayigh asserted that oral history can center often elided stories and peoples and highlight the need for social change.

Considering the systemic anti-Palestinian racism in/by the West, including the "un-narration" of Palestine and the systemic silencing and smearing of Palestinians and others who advocate for Palestinian liberation in public discursive spaces, educators may be hesitant to center Palestinian histories and narratives—even if they self-describe their pedagogical orientations as antiracist, anti-oppressive, decolonial, anticolonial, justice oriented, and/or liberatory.[15] This chapter gives insights into ways that educators might enact their commitments in relation to Palestine and Palestinians and remember that (history) education is, and always has been, political through the stories we choose to (not) tell. As Sayigh reminds us, "Oral history work is inherently political through its central impulse to raise silenced social categories—women, the working class, colonized groups—into the sphere of public knowledge."[16] Throughout this chapter, I contend that centering Palestinian oral histories and narratives can provide life-affirming counterstories to dominant (Euro/West-centric, colonial, racist, and misogynist) narratives in history education.

Before proceeding, it is important to stress that although I am a proud Palestinian woman and (grand)daughter of Nakba survivors, I am one Palestinian educator and scholar who was born and raised in the diaspora; I do not speak for or on behalf of Palestinians. Further, while I thread insights, resources, examples, and suggestions throughout this chapter, I am wary of placing thick borders around how Palestinian oral histories and narratives can be engaged with in history education. I believe that doing so could inadvertently reinscribe neoliberal, Euro/West-centric approaches to history education that Palestinian storytelling inherently and powerfully counters. However, I am simultaneously wary of leaving what I am arguing for so open to interpretation that others "use" Palestinian oral histories and narratives in ways that do not honor their liberatory intent. So, for now, I stress that Palestinian oral histories and narratives are not simply telling stories or narrating tales about Palestine and Palestinians. All that I have experienced, read, and studied shapes my knowledge and understanding of Palestinian oral histories and narratives as profoundly communal, intergenerational, ancestral, and embodied; rooted in our love of the land, our culture(s), and each other;

resisting historical and ongoing colonization, colonial mythologies, elimination, and erasure; truth-telling that teaches wisdoms, possibilities, steadfastness, and liberation; and reminding us that our knowledge and history did not begin and will not end with resisting colonization, colonial mythologies, elimination, and erasure. Palestinian oral histories and narratives are vital to reclaiming the past and living liberatory presents and futures.

CONTEXT

Close to thirty years after that social studies class, following decades of researching and reading about Palestine, I can confidently assert that the "education" my teacher believed I was missing (i.e., written texts of documented and archived historical records) has only served to reinforce my intergenerational knowledge. This is why, alongside many others, I purposely use the distinction between the terms "schooling" and "education."[17] For me, "schooling" describes the process of imparting—most often by teachers to students—dominant narratives that have been created, curated, and/or maintained by people and groups with institutional, systemic, and social power in buildings and institutions named schools. Schooling can be profoundly miseducative. Conversely, "education" is the process of relational and generative engagements with people, other beings, places, and texts over time—including oral texts—alongside onto-epistemological groundings.

Indeed, it has been only relatively recently that I regard my high school social studies teachers' words and actions that day not only as an example of educational malpractice but as a form of violence rooted in Euro/West-centric, colonial, and racist logics. Because of the work of several Palestinian scholars, activists, and educators, I am now able to name what I experienced in class that day as a specific form of racism—anti-Palestinian racism.[18] Dania Majid noted that anti-Palestinian racism "is a form of anti-Arab racism that silences, excludes, erases, stereotypes, defames or dehumanizes Palestinians or their narratives."[19]

Scholars are continuing to re/conceptualize anti-Palestinian racism as a systemic form of racism that is distinct from, yet intertwined with, anti-Arab and anti-Muslim racism.[20] Further, there is a growing body of work related to how anti-Muslim racism (often named Islamophobia) intersects with and diverges from anti-Arab racism and anti-Palestinian racism in different contexts.[21]

A growing number of publications outline anti-Palestinian school practices and other forms of racism that Palestinian children and youth experience in classrooms and schools worldwide.[22] Approximately three years ago, Desmond Cole outlined several examples of anti-Palestinian racism that students in a Toronto school board were forced to navigate, including how "students who object to history lessons that erase Palestinian existence are told they are antisemitic."[23] In early March 2023, during a multicultural day event at a kindergarten to grade nine school in Halifax, a group of Palestinian students were "reportedly singled-out and told to remove their Keffiyehs—traditional scarf-like garments that represent the Palestinian culture and identity" because, as they were reportedly told by an administrator who demanded they remove their keffiyehs, "It's a sign of war."[24]

The racism that Palestinian students encounter in schooling contexts is not limited to the cases I highlighted above. Hanadi Shatara identified ongoing silences related to (even the mention of) Palestine and Palestinians in social studies educational research and scholarship.[25] Further, in my current research alongside Palestinian Muslim youth and families into their schooling experiences, participants have shared numerous stories of being confronted with different forms of anti-Palestinian racism in classrooms and schools, including through silences, colonial mythologies, repression, and dehumanization. One mother participant, Yafa, discussed how her son was told he could not present about Palestine for a school project that specifically asked students to share more about their familial histories and cultures because Palestine is not "on the current political map." A youth participant, Jenin, expressed her frustration with school officials refusing to allow her to teach about the colonial violence Palestinians are subjected to, particularly in Masjid Al-Aqsa during Ramadan, in the school's "social justice club" because it could be seen as "antisemitic."[26] Upset as she shared this story, Jenin compared this reaction to her school social justice club's vocal support for Ukraine alongside other global issues of injustice and asserted, "It's like we're not even allowed to be Palestinian."

Thinking with the stories I've shared thus far, I ask educators to consider: What are the historical, ongoing, and future consequences when Palestinian children, youth, families, and communities are storied in schooling systems as liars, hateful, and/or dangerous for asserting that we exist, that we know our history, and that we demand liberation and justice? What are the historical, ongoing, and future consequences when our stories continue to be denied and elided by schooling systems and those with institutional and systemic power?

APPROACH TO THE PAST: PALESTINIAN ORAL AND INTERGENERATIONAL HISTORIES

> The memories of women, transmitted from mouth to ear, body to body, hand to hand, were the world's earliest archives.
>
> —Fatma Kassem[27]

Reflecting upon my intergenerational knowledge and education, I think again about my high school social studies teachers' words and how often Palestinian narratives and onto-epistemological knowledge have been silenced, dismissed as "biased," rejected, and erased in formal schooling contexts. I also think about how often teaching students to "think historically" has been used as the guiding framework in social studies and history education. As Maribel Santiago and Tadashi Dozono noted in their introduction to this book, the emphasis on teaching historical thinking skills inherently also emphasizes history as an individual and decontextualized *cognitive* process rather than as profoundly communal, contextual, and embodied. In *Decolonizing Methodologies*, Linda Tuhiwai Smith (Ngāti Awa, Ngāti Porou, Tūhourangi) asserted, "Knowledge and the power to define what counts as real knowledge lie at the epistemic core of colonialism."[28] She argued that this involves confronting Western academia's supremacist logics, including its "self-generating arrogance, its origin mythologies and the stories that it tells to reinforce its hegemony."[29] Thus, Smith asserted that "reclaiming history is a critical and essential aspect of decolonization."[30]

Part of this reclamation of history necessarily involves resisting Western academia's insistence on the written word as superior to oral traditions and other ways of knowing. As Smith emphasized, "Writing has been viewed as the mark of a superior civilization and other societies have been judged, by this view, to be incapable of thinking critically and objectively, or having distance from ideas and emotions."[31] For history education in particular, reclaiming history involves resisting pervasive dominant narratives that only those historical accounts that have been written (and otherwise documented) and archived can be trusted as "true" or "factual." This insistence on written documentation fails to acknowledge that archival materials are also largely dependent on memory, interpretation, and—most importantly—power. Those with power are typically those who have the means and opportunity to write, record, collect, document, curate, archive, and narrate "official" versions of history. As Lena Jayyusi emphasized, "It is important to note, however, that historical "records" themselves do not offer a pristine reflection of the world as it unfolded either. Are they not also subject to institutional (and state) interests, classifications that bow to particular epistemic and moral frames, to mistakes, blind spots and self-conscious omissions?"[32] Oral histories and oral history archives are thus not only counternarratives, they are also counterarchives; they not only counter the narrative of "official" colonial archives, they also counter the very notion of what traditionally counts as an archive.

This is particularly important given that Palestinian oral history is not only a way of preserving our memory, knowledge, and culture but vital for preserving our history as a people. As Masalha noted, "In the case of the Palestinian Nakba, oral history is not merely one choice of methodology. Rather its use can represent a decision as to whether to record any history at all."[33] Masalha clarified that this is because, as a predominantly rural society pre-Nakba, Palestinians who lived in agrarian areas (falaheen) constituted 66 percent of the population, and approximately 15 percent of Palestinians in these areas were literate in the written word. However, as Sayigh asserted, Palestinians "possessed a highly developed oral culture, in which all kinds of knowledge—methods of farming, property boundaries, genealogies, proverbs, folk poetry and stories, songs, myths, history—were transmitted orally."[34] Traditionally central to this historical and intergenerational oral transmission of knowledge, memory, and culture—what Farah Alkhammash referred to as "Palestinian oral literature"—were traveling storytellers, known as al-hakawati, who not only entertained their audiences but also ensured that Palestinians across different areas of Palestine were aware of current and historical events.[35] As Masalha asserted, "The powerful oral/aural culture of Palestine survived into the post-Nakba period. In the immediate post-catastrophe period the Arab tradition of storytelling in the form of al-hakawati (the storyteller) was deployed as a way of countering Zionist memoricide and toponymicide – the erasure of the material culture of Palestine and Palestinian cultural memory."[36] Yara Hawari similarly asserted that cross-generational transmission of memory and knowledge through storytelling has been a vital means of resistance against colonial physical and historical erasure and an essential method of keeping the memories of pre-Nakba Palestine as well as the knowledge of the Nakba alive in Palestinians over time.[37]

Reflecting upon the stories of Palestine that Sittee shared with me, including stories of unfathomable pain and trauma as a Nakba survivor, I think of how Palestinian women, in particular, have been integral to the intergenerational preservation of Palestinian histories, knowledge, memories, and culture. Highlighting the voices and experiences of women Nakba survivors living in Gaza, Barbara Bill and Ghada Ageel emphasized how intergenerational transmission of knowledge, culture, and memory is

> a deeply significant site for resisting policies of elimination and erasure. Often, such resistance work takes place within families, and, in particular, through women. Stories of lost homes are handed down from generation to generation and repeated time and again, preserving the names of lost villages and towns, detailing former landholdings, passing on deeds, and recounting traditions and tales about "the ancestors, everyday life, the harvests, and even quarrels." When asked where they are from, most of the children of Palestinian refugee families will state the name of a village lost generations ago.[38]

In *Palestinian Women: Narrative Histories and Gendered Memory*, Fatma Kassem similarly explored the oral testimonies of Palestinian women Nakba survivors and asserted, "This multi-generational engagement in storytelling indicates that the private home functions as a site of commemoration that celebrates Palestinian history, heritage, culture, and memory."[39] For Palestinians, then, our homes are often "a site of resistance that protects Palestinian history (as narrative and memory) from oblivion," and this communal site of commemoration and resistance has been sustained by Palestinian women in different ways across familial and community contexts, time, places, and generations.[40]

The oral storytelling of Palestinian women survivors of the Nakba has, however, too often been silenced, omitted, or rejected in Nakba histories, schooling, and history education. Sayigh argued that Palestinian women's stories have been marginalized because history is too often "defined as knowledge of events, from which experience, especially women's experience, is rigorously excluded."[41] As I discussed in the introduction to this chapter, refusing to acknowledge Palestinian oral histories and narratives is prolific in Western schooling and is rooted in anti-Palestinian racism. The silencing, denial, and erasure of Palestinian knowledge and history is rampant in Western countries in general, including the settler-colonial nation-states of the US and Canada—two colonial nation-states that are complicit in, and actively fund and/or otherwise materially support, Israel's colonization of Palestine and violence against Palestinians.[42] The historical and ongoing silencing and erasure of Palestinian (oral) histories and narratives, and those of Palestinian women in particular, must be countered through a radically different and honest history education.

IMPLICATIONS FOR PRACTICE: TOWARD A RADICALLY DIFFERENT HISTORY EDUCATION

Sometimes I reflect on that racist experience in social studies class and think that not much has changed since then. I think of the experiences of anti-Palestinian racism in classrooms and schools that research participants shared with me and numerous accounts of anti-Palestinian racism in the news and social media, and it can sometimes feel overwhelmingly bleak. However, I remind myself of historical and ongoing resistances by Palestinians in Palestine and across the diaspora. I remind myself of the countless people worldwide who are in solidarity with Palestinians and who are organizing alongside us for collective liberation and the liberation of Palestine. I remind myself of the stories that Sittee and other Palestinian women and Nakba survivors have lived and re/told across time, places, and generations to educate about our history, land, culture, and righteous struggle for liberation.

It is important to note that not everyone has the opportunity to learn directly from the embodied intergenerational knowledge of Palestinians and those who survived the Nakba for many different reasons, including the fact that many Nakba survivors have passed away. Further, while many Nakba survivors have re/told their stories of experiences, many survivors of the Nakba chose not to share their stories because of ongoing trauma.[43]

Further, embracing Palestinian oral histories and narratives in history education does not mean entirely eschewing written histories; it should not be regarded as either/or but rather both/and. Sayigh argued for the production of written literature about Palestinian history for children in particular because, even when Palestinian children do have access to intergenerational familial histories, they must be able to situate this history within an overarching popular national framework of Palestinian liberation and relate this knowledge to other global struggles against colonialism and imperialism. Sayigh asserted, "Scattered since 1948 across diverse educational systems, Palestinians have been unable to control their education or construct an authentic curriculum."[44] Sayigh argued that education that "would include histories that explain their situation, and depict past resistances" is especially vital for Palestinian children, and in particular Palestinian children in Palestine and refugee camps, because of the "deep need of self-knowledge, especially of their history of resistance, in their long and arduous struggle against colonialist dispossession."[45]

How, then, might educators move toward a radically different and honest history education and embrace Palestinian narratives and oral histories, knowledges, and traditions? How might educators engage in this work in the face of the Israeli occupation regime's ongoing genocide in Gaza and ongoing colonization, ethnic cleansing, displacement, dispossession, apartheid, sophicide, scholasticide, and epistemicide across Palestine?[46]

Alongside honoring the knowledge of Palestinian students, families, educators, and community members in their own contexts, educators must center the narratives and testimonies of Palestinians—especially Palestinians living in Palestine right now. Educators in elementary, middle, and senior schooling contexts might be unsure of how to do this as they are often required to adhere to state-mandated curricula. However, as I often remind pre-service teachers in our social studies methods courses, educators typically have the professional autonomy to decide *how* they would like to approach teaching about the mandated curricula. For example, many social studies curricula include an acknowledgment of the need to learn and teach about current events. Educators can teach about how historical events, narratives, and processes are connected to current events in Palestine, particularly the ongoing genocide of Palestinians in Gaza and colonial violence and oppression across Palestine, by posing critical questions such as, *What are the historical roots of this violence? How can we learn more about these historical roots? Whose narratives and experiences should we center as we learn more about this? Why?* Further, many mandated curricula include required content areas (sometimes named as standards, competencies, or objectives) that could serve as entryways to making powerful connections to Palestinian histories and narratives, including those related to identity, family, culture(s), power and perspectives, human rights, historical people and events, types of migration, genocide and other historical atrocities, imperialism, and (settler) colonialism. Some curricula explicitly require students to learn about "the 1948 Arab-Israeli War." Educators in these contexts must not only teach about and through Palestinian (oral) histories and narratives, they must also problematize the framings, silences, and erasures within the mandated curricula.

For historical Palestinian narratives and testimonies, alongside Palestinian oral histories that have been recorded in written form (some are referenced in this chapter), there are multiple Palestinian oral history counterarchives and helpful websites:

- The American University of Beirut's (AUB) Palestinian Oral History Archive is an online database that includes over 1000 hours of testimonies from Nakba survivors.[47] The AUB's Palestine Oral History Map is an accompanying resource that helps to map out and visualize many of these testimonies.[48]
- The Nakba Archive was created by, for, and with Palestinian refugee communities in Lebanon.[49]
- Duke University's Palestinian Oral History Project (2017–2020).[50]
- While it is not entirely dedicated to counterarchiving Palestinian oral histories, Project 48 includes videos of Nakba survivor testimonies alongside lesson plans, presentations, and galleries of historical images and artifacts for teaching about Palestinian history, with a focus on the Nakba.[51]
- Similarly, the Teach Palestine website includes many videos of Palestinians bearing witness and providing testimony alongside lesson plans and other resources.[52]

However, it is important to note that engaging with these histories in the classroom must be approached with a spirit of humility, thoughtfulness, and care. Palestinian oral histories and testimonies must be honored as profoundly political acts of truth-telling and resistance while simultaneously being wakeful to how every single testimony holds unquantifiable pain and strength that reverberates across time, places, families, communities, and generations.

Moreover, the act of recording Palestinian oral history and testimonies has changed their very nature because, as I asserted in the introduction, Palestinian oral histories and narratives are inherently relational and communal. While the archived oral histories and testimonies I highlighted were often recorded in familial and communal contexts, the recordings can be accessed and used by anyone—including by those with arrogant or even nefarious intent. If educators invite recorded Nakba survivor testimonies into their classrooms, these testimonies must be approached as a form of *living knowledge* that was recorded in a particular context by a particular group of people with truth-telling intent and, most importantly, with a Nakba survivor who is bearing witness to horrific colonial violence.[53] They should never be misused as a decontextualized teaching "tool," intellectualized to teach "skills" related to "historical thinking," and/or misused in any other dehumanizing way that reduces the fact that the survivors are real people who are bearing witness and giving testimony to their experiences—including those laden with the horrors and traumas of colonial violence. When recorded Palestinian oral histories and testimonies are engaged with in history education classes, educators must stress the importance of honoring those bearing witness and their testimonies.

Importantly, attempts to appear "neutral" or "apolitical" or to teach in ways that ignore power imbalances by storying "both sides" as equal must be eschewed when engaging with Palestinians' oral histories and their historical and ongoing experiences of colonial violence. Teaching in radically honest ways necessarily entails naming and educating about the ongoing colonization of Palestine and the ethnic cleansing, displacement, dispossession, genocide, and oppression of Palestinians. Moreover, Shatara recommended the following for educators committed to learning and teaching about Palestine in formal schooling contexts: explicitly saying Palestine and Palestinians as we are often silenced or erased in schooling systems and dominant narratives; remembering that although Palestinians are connected, we are diverse and not a monolith; including everyday Palestinians and Palestinian culture and joy (not only the injustice and violence we face); and reading and following Palestinian scholars, organizations, and activists and their allies (Shatara included multiple examples on pages 78 to 80).[54]

Alongside embracing Palestinian oral histories and narratives as onto-epistemological and political acts of resistance against the violence of colonial silencing, elimination, and erasure, educators would do well to heed Masalha's words when educating about Palestine and Palestinian history: "Remembrance should be an act of hope, liberation and decolonisation. Edward Said once argued that to write more truthfully about what happened in 1948 is not merely to practise professional historiography; it is also a profoundly moral act of redemption and a struggle for justice and for a better world."[55]

CLOSING THOUGHTS: RE/TELLING HONEST AND HOPEFUL STORIES IN HISTORY EDUCATION

Throughout this chapter, I have stressed the need to re/tell radically different stories in history education. I have stressed the imperative of re/telling stories that reject colonial mythologies and the pervasive elisions of Palestinian narratives and histories. I continue to stress that we must re/tell radically honest and hopeful stories—stories that embrace Palestinian oral histories and narratives—in history education and beyond.

CHAPTER 7

Centering Pinxy Narratives: Kuwentos and Kuwentuhan in History Education

JOCYL SACRAMENTO AND LAUREN ARZAGA DAUS

We were never fans of history education. History was a class—second period—where we memorized dates, people, and places of the past. We remember seeing a paragraph in our history textbooks referring to Filipinos as the "Little Brown Brothers" of the United States. The absence of Filipina/x/o American history within textbooks taught us that our stories were not valuable nor significant to learn. We never saw ourselves as part of history as students in K–12 education. We saw history as an object to be studied rather than seeing ourselves as subjects within a broader socio-historical-political context. As education scholars today, we recognize that the subtractive schooling[1] we experienced in our youth was part of a larger educational project designed to reproduce and maintain society and the status quo.[2] As we reflect on our experiences with history and learning Filipina/x/o American history, more specifically, we realize that our initial teachings and learnings came from our communities and families, primarily through the cultural practices of kuwentos and kuwentuhan, or stories and storytelling. Through these practices, we began to acknowledge the necessity of learning history and how history, the government, and the economy have shaped our lived experiences. In other words, kuwentos and kuwentuhan transformed our relationship with history and history education.

Jocyl's Kuwento

My introduction to Filipina/x/o American history happened in Seattle, Washington (Dumawish land), in the summer of 1998. I was sixteen years old, and it was the first time my parents let me fly on a plane without them to visit my cousins Kuya Rene and Rey, my Uncle Renato, and Auntie Tina. During my two-week stay in Seattle, my Kuya Rene and Rey brought me to significant Filipina/x/o sites in the city, which included José Rizal Park, tours of the University of Washington—where Kuya Rene had taken Asian American studies—and to the annual festival called Pista sa Nayon or "Pista" for short. As a young teenage Pinay, this was my introduction to Filipina/x/o America. At the time, my cousins DJ'd local events, so I got to tag along to the weddings, debuts, Kasama hip-hop dance practices, and church gatherings, where they were expected to provide music and lighting. I also remember Kuya Rene wearing a shirt that said "BROWN" in bold letters. At Pista, he even bought me a khaki bucket hat with the embroidered word "PINAY." My conversations with Kuya Rene that summer were some of the first instances that developed my critical consciousness of Filipinas/xs/os and racialization.

In some strange way, I felt at home in Seattle as my cousins talked story about their lives and the communities they belonged to. Before this trip, I knew my father's point of entry to the United States was the city of Seattle, but little did I know that my father was one of many Filipinos who found their way to the Emerald City. My father was a product of chain migration. My Uncle Renato was the first in my family to immigrate to the United States as an engineer who found work with Boeing in Seattle in the late 1960s. He petitioned for my Lola and Lolo to migrate, who then brought my father over to the States. Years later, in my Intro to Asian American Studies class, I made the connection that my family's presence in the US was a result of the family reunification preferences of the Hart-Celler Act, also known as the Immigration and Nationality Act of 1965.

Lauren's Kuwento

Growing up, I was aware that I was Pinay, but I never really knew what that meant until I was thirteen. In September 2003, my older cousins and siblings brought me to the annual Festival of Philippine Arts and Culture (FPAC) at Point Fermin Park in San Pedro, California (Tongva land). There, I became exposed to the most Filipinas/xs/os I had ever seen in one place. I felt so proud to be Pinay, as I was surrounded by my history and culture in the form of food, dance, music, clothing, and community. This inspired me to learn more and even share with my friends about my Filipina/x/o history and identity. I looked forward to FPAC every year because it was a space where I felt a sense of belonging as a Pinay. I would stop by every clothing vendor and buy T-shirts that had the Philippines flag colors of red, blue, and yellow or T-shirts that said "Pinay" and be excited to wear them to school, especially during Filipina/o American History Month (FAHM) in October. I would even post daily facts about historical events or Filipina/x/o American celebrities during FAHM on my MySpace Bulletin Board. This was my way of sharing my knowledge and connecting with other Filipinas/xs/os outside of the classroom space.

When I got to high school, I wanted to expand my learning by reading books written by Filipino authors. During a Friday afternoon at Cerritos Towne Center, after taking studio pictures with my friends (which was basically a ritual every other Friday after school), I walked into the Borders bookstore and just straight up asked one of the employees, "Do you have any Filipino books?" Asking this question out loud made me feel like I should've asked the question differently, or that it was a dumb question to ask, or that I should've just searched for the books myself. Reflecting on this moment now makes me realize that I probably felt this way because I grew up reading books by white authors—so I thought, "Why WOULD they have Filipino books?" But the employee actually walked me over to a section, pulled a book off the shelves, said, "This is the only book we have," and handed me a gray book that had a Filipino man etched in black and gray ink on the cover. The book was called America Is in the Heart *by Carlos Bulosan.* America Is in the Heart *ended up being the first book that taught me about my own history and sparked my interest in education and Ethnic studies. In reading about how Filipinas/os experienced racism and poverty in America, I was able to make connections to my ancestors' and my family's experiences. It was the first time I saw myself in what I was learning, and what I was learning was not in the classroom.*

In our chapter, we share how kuwentos and kuwentuhan are essential tools that center Pinxy narratives that are often omitted in social science classrooms. We start with the origins of kuwentos and kuwentuhan. We then share examples of how we have engaged in kuwentos as a pedagogy in the classroom and kuwentuhan as a research method to historicize Filipina/x/o American experiences. Lastly, we conclude with offerings on engaging in kuwentos and kuwentuhan as educators and scholars rooted in Ethnic studies.

CONTEXT

Origins of Kuwentos and Kuwentuhan

Kuwentos and kuwentuhan come from practices in the Philippines that were influenced by over three hundred years of Spanish colonialism. Kuwento is a Tagalog

FIGURE 7.1 "Kuwento" in pre-colonial Philippine script Baybayin

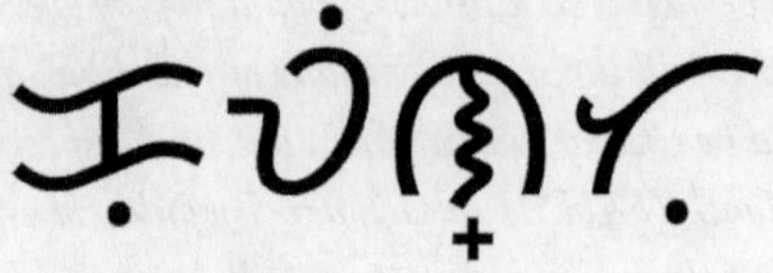

word that means "story" and draws from the Spanish word "cuento." In the pre-colonial Philippine script known as Baybayin, kuwento (shown in figure 7.1), is pronounced *koo-wen-toh*. Kuwentuhan is the process of sharing or collecting kuwentos, or storytelling. This process is based on oral traditions of re-membering[3] and has often been used to share Philippine folk literature.[4] Educators have brought the familial tradition of kuwentuhan to the classroom to engage students in learning Filipina/x/o American history.[5] These stories are part of our Filipina/x/o linguistic and familial capital, as they encapsulate "the recounting of oral histories" and "cultural knowledges nurtured among *familia*."[6] Kuwentuhan provides students and teachers the opportunity to draw connections between past and present experiences while placing our narratives within a larger socio-historical-political context. Reflecting on the relationship between narrative and identity, Roderick Daus-Magbual asserts:

> Narrative identity involves the orientation of time, history, and the formation of identity in relationship to grand narratives and possible counternarratives. . . . The embodiment of these historical narratives shape[s] people's identities to become storied beings. As storied beings, we manifest into the narrative that is imposed to the dominant culture. It can also potentially serve as a space and process in creating new notions of self by understanding one's history.[7]

Sharing kuwentos shifts the identity of a storyteller to a storied being. Pinxys have historically embodied the dominant culture to fit into the US narrative because of the rarity of learning about our counternarratives in K–12 history classes. Kuwentos allow us to process our experiences as storied beings who have the agency to resist traditional and oppressive ways of learning and create liberatory spaces for understanding our history from our people's perspectives. Sharing kuwentos is a form of resistance to reclaim,[8] reflect, and re-member stories that are often omitted from traditional history classroom spaces.

While kuwento means story, kuwentuhan is the act of telling stories. Valerie Francisco developed kuwentuhan as a method of talk story with Filipino migrants.[9] Combining kuwentuhan and Participatory Action Research (PAR), Francisco argued that in sharing their individual stories, Filipino migrants made explicit connections to the larger collective experiences of forced migration. Francisco collaborated with the migrant workers to engage in kuwentuhan, with the purpose of creating a space where they felt safe and brave enough to exchange their stories. With this in mind, engaging in kuwentuhan should be a collaborative process with and amongst Pinxy students. In the next section, we share how kuwentos can be utilized as a pedagogical framework in history education.

APPROACH TO THE PAST: ELEMENTS AND PRACTICES OF KUWENTUHAN

Rose Ann Gutierrez, Hazel Piñon, and Marie Trisha Valmocena used kuwentuhan as a research method to illuminate the experiences of Filipino students who are undocumented. From their research process, they found three elements of kuwentuhan: collective storying and memorying, co-producing knowledge through Filipino talk story, and a generational language.[10] They recognize kuwentuhan as a tool for Filipina/x/o students to reclaim their history and identities in educational spaces, particularly in higher education. We recognize kuwentuhan as a form of praxis[11] in which storied beings engage in these three elements. In the following sections, we share how each of the elements looks in practice.

Historicizing Filipina/x/o American Experiences Through Collective Storying and Memorying

The first element of kuwentuhan is collective storying and memorying, which describes how individuals tell their own kuwentos and are able to connect them to a larger collective story.[12] With this, students are able to historicize their experiences, which have often been omitted or misrepresented by dominant narratives in history education, and imprint themselves as part of history. Engaging in oral histories, especially with family members, is a way for Pinxy students to historicize their experiences. Like many students, we did not learn about the concept and practice of oral histories until we pursued higher education. As Asian American Studies students at San Francisco State University—the birthplace of the first College of Ethnic Studies—we were introduced to the liberatory educational spaces we longed for. Taking courses with Filipina/o professors such as Daniel Phil Gonzales, Sunny Vergara, Danilo Begonia, Irene Duller, Allyson Tintiangco-Cubales, and the late Dawn Bohulano Mabalon, we learned the parallel struggles and survival stories of Black, Indigenous, and People of Color (BIPOC) and the importance of interweaving our histories and identities with others. Specifically, we learned how oral histories create possibilities for Filipina/x/o Americans to forge their experiences from the margins to the center of history education. Oral histories can take the form of kuwentuhan.

As young Pinays, we never really heard our parents talk about their experiences growing up in the Philippines and immigrating to the US. However, after taking Ethnic Studies courses in college, we learned about how difficult it can be for Filipina/x/o immigrants to want to share their stories because of the historical/intergenerational/ancestral trauma they inherit.[13] "As descendants do not directly experience traumas of their ancestors, the traumas may become decontextualized from their original time and place."[14] For Lauren, learning about historical trauma provided her with a new understanding, as well as an entry point for her to create a space with her parents to share their stories as a way to humanize their experiences and engage in their healing process. With this, Lauren chose to do oral histories with her parents, along with one of her aunties and one of her uncles, and write about their experiences as post-1965 Filipina/o immigrants for her undergraduate thesis.

Similarly, lessons of chain migration inspired Jocyl to engage in kuwento with her mother and father about how they migrated to the US. Kuwentuhan allowed Jocyl to humanize her family's experiences while simultaneously recognizing her family's story as part of a larger historical context. As Jocyl mentioned in her kuwento, the Immigration and Nationality Act of 1965 allowed for family reunification. As it was initially meant to progressively change the immigration quota system and remove the discriminatory restrictions on visas, its purpose was also to allow people to immigrate to the US based on their skills and familial relationships with US citizens.[15] Many Filipinas/os took advantage of this new legislation for economic opportunities in the US, which inspired us to learn more about our family's history.

From engaging in kuwentuhan with our families, we were able to make explicit connections between what we learned in our college classes and our family's stories. This allowed for us to historicize our family's experiences as Filipina/o immigrants who came to the US. We learned about the challenges our families faced when searching for employment opportunities and raising their children in a new environment while adapting to the "American" culture. We also listened to kuwentos we never heard before, which enabled us to contextualize our family's behavioral traits and understand why our family members do the things they do in the ways that they do. In sharing our own kuwentos with one another, we learned that our experiences as second-generation Pinays are linked, despite growing up in different cities and neighborhoods.

Engaging in these oral histories mirrored the process of kuwentuhan because we were also able to learn more about ourselves and historicize our experiences as Pinay daughters of Filipina/o immigrants. This particular process of kuwentuhan marked the beginning of our families taking ownership of their narratives, connecting with themselves, and learning to embody a life of liberation.[16] Because kuwentuhan can be practiced as a form of historicizing and collective storying and memorying, it can also be seen as an act of resistance to white colonial narratives that tend to omit the perspectives and experiences of Filipinas/x/os.

Teachers Cocreating Knowledge Through Kuwentuhan

The second element of kuwentuhan is co-producing knowledge. Kuwentuhan is a cultural practice for people, especially Filipinas/xs/os, to share their epistemologies and how they understand what they know. This is possible when people have cultivated relationships grounded in the understanding that their struggles are tied together.[17] The practice of kuwentuhan provides an opportunity for people to access their experiences through time, space, and relationships with others.[18] Kuwentuhan, as a praxis, disrupts canonical ways of doing research, such as interviews, by allowing the researcher to meaningfully collaborate and exist with their participants, rather than being seen as separate from them. Kuwentuhan challenges researchers to break power relationships in that it develops space for researchers and participants to be cocreators of knowledge.

In December 2022, Lauren engaged in a virtual kuwentuhan with former colleagues that centered their experiences participating in interdisciplinary teaching on Zoom during the 2020–2021 school year.[19] The overarching questions that comprised the virtual kuwentuhan were: How did we sustain our wellness alongside our students during distance learning? What is the importance of engaging in grief as educators? Referencing "we" and "our" in the questions denotes that Lauren did not only see herself as the researcher but as a participant in the kuwentuhan. During the kuwentuhan, they were not expected to follow specific guidelines or formal ways of talking. Instead, a circular exchange of stories and questions happened organically, "allowing [them] to build from one another's experiences and perspectives to make sense of their own."[20] Despite not seeing or talking with each other for several months, they were still comfortable enough to embody vulnerability and joy during their kuwentuhan because of the strong relationships they had built with each other over the years.

Kuwentuhan as Ancestral Wisdom

The third element is the ability to see kuwentuhan as a generational language passed down from ancestral wisdom. Kuwentuhan is a generational language in two ways: "(1) the ability to speak Tagalog and understand the nuances of *kuwentuhan* embedded within the language of Tagalog and (2) the inability to speak Tagalog, yet still possess the ability to understand the nuances of [kuwentuhan] as an embodied practice."[21] Whether a person is Filipina/x/o or not, one can engage in kuwentuhan as a way of preserving and passing down the wisdom and practices from their ancestors. Because of this, kuwentuhan can be utilized as both a tool and a space. In the next section, we share how we collectively created a virtual space where we grounded ourselves in the element of kuwentuhan, representing ancestral wisdom.

In the summer of 2020, we developed a virtual space to respond to national and local movements. Created because of our dear friend, the late Dr. Gwen Agustin-Nodora, and inspired by third-wave feminism,[22] Pin@y Educational Partnerships' Praxis-Oriented Development Series (PEP PODS) is a space for critical consciousness-raising among school and community practitioners committed to combating anti-Black racism, ableism, and sexism in their praxis. We expand on the concept of hybridity as a catalyst for third spaces.[23] Our third space also allowed for the imagining and strengthening of solidarities and empathy across racial groups during a time of isolation due to the COVID-19 global pandemic and state-sanctioned violence. Engaging in hybridity has allowed us to explore the complexities of our identities as school and community practitioners in relation to BIPOC-led national and local movements. PEP PODS offers a praxis in developing third spaces that coalesce our identities and pedagogies, emphasizing the importance of community, care, and collaboration. This speaks to the ancestral wisdom we are able to re-member and share with each other.

PEP PODS mirrors kuwentuhan as we dialogue, reflect, and analyze to make meaning of our relational experiences. Drawing from our past virtual kuwentuhan sessions, we expanded our understanding of racial justice and disability justice to inform our praxis and pedagogies. We created PEP PODS to respond to the need for school and community practitioners to have a collective space where they could make sense of their identities and commitments to social justice in the midst of community grief during the summer 2020 uprisings. Since then, PEP PODS participants have collectively read *Freedom Dreams* by Robin D.G. Kelley, *Me and White Supremacy: Combat Racism, Change the World, and Become a Good Ancestor* by Layla Saad, and *Care Work: Dreaming Disability Justice* by Leah Lakshmi Piepzna-Samarasinha. These texts provided frameworks to situate our work and challenged us to return to our purpose, reflect on our commitments, and reimagine our roles as school and community practitioners in the context of our collective grief. We also learned how historical legacies of oppression diverge because of different historical contexts, yet how our experiences are interconnected through the resistance we embody in our present-day work and the solidarity built between Communities of Color that came before us.

PEP PODS, as a third space, has been instrumental in welcoming and centering our humanity as we continue to endure oppressive and inconducive working environments. Kuwentuhan allowed us the space to humanize ourselves and connect our work to larger social movements. Despite experiencing cultural taxation[24] and racial battle fatigue,[25] we continue to engage in this space because it serves as a reminder of the many possibilities that can exist outside of educational spaces and workplaces. PEP PODS is an example of a counter space that allows school and community practitioners to share our ancestral wisdom, engage in humanizing dialogue, and build solidarity across various contexts—historically scarce opportunities for BIPOC students and practitioners in education.

IMPLICATIONS FOR PRACTICE

Kuwentos can be used as a pedagogical praxis to engage students in understanding stories of people, places, and times and how the stories have shaped their experiences and the experiences of their families and communities.[26] Simultaneously, students learn how they, too, can shape kuwentos and kuwentuhan. Kuwentos are "based on (aspects of) actual events retold and reconstructed in the presence of others."[27] Korina Jocson asserts that kuwentos are a necessary pedagogical tool for Ethnic Studies, multicultural, and antiracist education because they are used to provide counternarratives to dominant understandings of the collective history one typically learns within traditional history education spaces.[28] In her study of the use of kuwento as pedagogy in a Filipino Heritage Studies class, Jocson recognized kuwento as

- monologic and dialogic (between teacher and student or among students);
- occurring in the past, present, and future (subject matter spanning a historical continuum);
- brief (speakers taking turns) and at length; and
- oral (versus written or visual) and nonoral in form.[29]

Notice that these aspects of kuwento do not require that the teacher should know how to speak Tagalog or be Filipina/x/o. However, if a teacher were to use kuwento as a pedagogical tool, it is important they know that students carry linguistic practices that are meant to be valued and expanded on in their education. When incorporated in the classroom, kuwento is a way to educe knowledge from students and teachers and engage in meaning-making processes in which new knowledge is co-constructed. For example, this can happen when the teacher poses a question to the students. The objective of posing a question is to assess students' understanding of the topic and what they bring to the conversation. This is a way of creating opportunities and spaces for students to engage in their education meaningfully.

Kuwentuhan is an epistemological exercise where students examine how they have come to understand a particular topic. Students share kuwentos of their experiences and knowledge related to a specific topic. This approach to guiding students "draws on the strengths of its participants."[30] Such an approach invites students to recognize that they are active in defining ideas and concepts, that their voices and perspectives are valued. According to the History-Social Science Content Standards for California Public Schools,[31] students in grades nine through twelve are expected to learn and demonstrate certain analytical skills, such as comparing past and present events and analyzing how change happens in different contexts. Kuwentuhan is a practice that involves collecting, telling, and interpreting kuwentos as primary sources. This process allows students to further their critical reflection on historical events and social science analysis skills. Educators outside of California can strengthen their defense of using kuwentuhan by familiarizing themselves with history and social science education standards in their region.

In Jocyl's "Pinayism: Filipina Experiences and Activism" course, students engage with kuwento as they learn Filipina/x/o American Studies from the perspective of Pinay counterstorytelling. Students are assigned kuwento projects where they learn the skills to collect kuwentos. They also consider how to use kuwento within an educational context in a curriculum project for the course. In their kuwento project, students are instructed to engage in kuwentuhan with someone who identifies as a woman, non-binary, or gender-conforming Pinay, Pinxy, F/Pilipina/x, or F/Pilipina/x American living in the United States. The goal of the assignment is to analyze significant events in Pinay/Pinxy lives and discuss these events within the context of the themes of Pinayism.[32] While a majority of students who have taken this class thus far identify as Pina/x/oy, Filipina/x/o, or Filipina/x/o American, there are students in the class who do not identify as Pinay/Pinxy and do not know anyone to interview. When this happens, Jocyl connects them with a Pinay faculty or staff member within the campus community, or they choose to interview one of their Pinay classmates. The intention of this assignment is to center Pinay narratives and experiences. Students are guided by the following definition of Kuwento-Kuwentuhan:

> Kuwento in Tagalog is borrowed from the word cuento in Spanish, both meaning "story." Kuwentos are counterstories and counternarratives of resistance, resilience, and radical possibilities. It is also a research and teaching method to analyze feminisms of Color, like Pinayism. For this assignment, I'd like you to illuminate Pin[a/x]y experiences and how Pin[a/x]ys navigate hate found in cis-heteropatriarchy, white supremacy, classism, and other systems of oppression and exploitation. I'd also like you to share and examine Pinay joy and liberation through the primary sources of Pin[a/x]y experience.
>
> According to Korina Jocson, kuwentos are "not simply about sharing stories but also about the nature in which the stories take place."[33] In other words, kuwentos do not exist in a vacuum. They are "produced, reproduced, and recycled as a consequence of social interactions."[34] In this manner, the social, the political, and the personal intertwine as the recounting of kuwentos also acknowledges lived realities, entangled and often relational experiences that cannot be understood in isolation.
>
> How does your kuwento capture the Pinayist themes of "struggle, survival, service, sisterhood, solidarity, strength, self-love, and shapeshifting?"[35] Pinayism centralizes the experiences of Pinays because we are so often marginalized in any and every field of study.

Kuwentos are also related to oral history in that oral history is a process of collecting personal accounts or stories. Oral history is also a practice of passing down these stories by verbally sharing them with others. Collecting kuwentos and/or oral histories is a social science method where we gain evidence from a primary source.

The kuwento project happens over the course of seven weeks. The seven-week schedule is based on an asynchronous course (table 7.1). This schedule can be adjusted depending on how often students meet for the class.[36]

TABLE 7.1 The kuwento project

Week	*Task*
Week 1	• Identify a Pin[a/x]y to interview, reach out, and schedule kuwentuhan. (If you do not know any Pin[a/x]ys, the instructor will connect you with someone in the community.)
Week 2	• Brainstorm questions to ask during kuwentuhan exchange. These questions will help guide you, but feel free to ask follow-up questions that may come up during the kuwento. Remember you will be analyzing significant events in their lives, so be sure to develop questions that will help them talk about specific events. • If time permits, practice questions with fellow classmates or have someone ask you the questions to ensure that you receive the type of response you are looking for. Revise questions if needed.
Week 3	• Engage in kuwentuhan (process of storytelling, sharing stories). • Transcribe kuwento (if you are able to record interviews on Zoom, Zoom will transcribe for you). Begin to "code" the quotes from the transcript into themes. • Submit transcript and quotes organized into different themes.
Week 4	• Outline and write your kuwento. • Identify texts (readings, videos, podcasts, guest speakers, poetry, etc. from the course) that relate to the person's life or help explain the experiences in the kuwento. Include texts (through paraphrasing or quotes) in your outline. You will need to include at least 3 citations from the course material in your written kuwentuhan. How might their experiences relate to your own experience? • Write introduction, body paragraphs, and conclusion. • Submit first draft of kuwento.
Week 5	• Peer feedback • Using the rubric, provide feedback to a peer. How could they strengthen their kuwento?
Week 6	• Incorporate feedback into your kuwentuhan. • Submit revised final draft.
Week 7	• Prepare kuwento presentation. • Record 5–7-minute oral presentation.

Practicing kuwentuhan provides students the opportunity to link Pin[a/x]y experiences to socio-historical-political phenomena, which enables them to recognize collective experiences. This is particularly true when students witness the kuwentos written by other students and start to make connections between the various kuwentos presented in a class, whether it relates to migration experience, labor practices, or familial dynamics/expectations. The kuwento project also helps students realize their agency in writing history and seeing their family or community members' stories as part of a larger historical legacy.

Educators who wish to introduce kuwentuhan in the classroom should be mindful of student and teacher positionalities with regard to power relations. Additionally, kuwentuhan draws from first-person perspectives and operates under the assumption of pluriversality rather than universal truth.[37] In other words, different communities experience socio-historical-political phenomena in various ways. Kuwentuhan helps to illuminate the perspectives of those whose narratives are often erased or neglected from traditional history education spaces. In the following sections, we shift to how kuwentuhan is a praxis for historicizing experiences and disrupting traditional ways of engaging in research.

Kuwentuhan as Praxis

Storytelling has been a cultural practice in many BIPOC communities. Because it incites meaningful ways to learn about people's experiences and perspectives, storytelling has been utilized as a method that disrupts the colonial ways of engaging in research. For example, pláticas and testimonios, which are rooted in Chicana and Latina Feminist epistemologies, are humanizing processes for researchers and participants to be recognized as collaborators and to engage in meaningful dialogue with each other.[38] Similarly, Hawai'ian and Indigenous researchers use talk story as a form of communication and meaning-making.[39] In relation, kuwentuhan is a form of Filipino talk story that "incorporates other people's experiences as an individual conveys one's own story."[40] Kuwentuhan allows storytellers to become storied beings who embody kapwa, the Tagalog word that unifies "self" and "others," thus recognizing a shared identity.[41] Because kuwentuhan allows for the weaving of individual stories, storied beings are able to collectively build a shared identity that has the potential to create counter possibilities of learning, being, and doing.

CLOSING THOUGHTS

Lauren's Kuwento

In my tenth-grade United States History class, my teacher assigned a final project that required us to present on "well-known" historical figures. She gave us a list of people to choose from; however, I told her that I wanted to present on someone else: Carlos Bulosan. With a confused look on my teacher's face, she replied, "Who is that? I've never heard of him." I told her that he was a Filipino immigrant who wrote America Is in the Heart, *a story about the struggles of Filipinas/os who came to the US in the 1930s, in search of a better life. With the class completely silent and my teacher still confused, she said, "It doesn't seem like he is a well-known figure, and he's not American. You need to pick someone who is, preferably from the list I gave you." The rejection made my heart pound because it was the first time I truly questioned American schooling.*

After having my identity pushed to the margins, I ended up presenting on Ludwig van Beethoven, someone I did not see any connection to whatsoever. I decided to be as creative as possible, so on my presentation day, I came dressed in one of my dad's gray suits and his pair of dark, mahogany brown dress shoes (please take this time to picture a short Brown girl dressed in oversized clothing). I captured everyone's attention as I took the identity of Beethoven, preaching about his "American" story, with his symphonies lightly playing in the background. After this experience, I was even more eager to learn about my Filipina/x/o American history and become active in sharing the stories of my people. Although I felt a disconnect in my education, I also felt the need to prove people wrong and put myself out there when I had the chance. As a quiet, passive student, I used oral presentations to engage my classmates and teachers in my misunderstood identity.

Lauren's kuwento is an explicit example of why kuwentos and kuwentuhan are important for Pinxy students in history education. This experience taught her that her Filipina/x/o American history and identity did not matter because she was not important enough to be in the history books, let alone truthfully represented. It was not until she took her first Ethnic studies class at SFSU that she saw herself in the curriculum. However, students should not have to wait until they pursue higher education (if they do) to learn about themselves and tell their stories.

Jocyl's Kuwento

Halfway through the school year, while teaching high school Filipina/x/o American Studies, the school board's agenda included a resolution to institutionalize Ethnic studies across the district. As students, parents, teachers, and community members filled the board meeting room, a former Pinay student approached me and shared that she wanted to say something during public comment but wasn't sure what to say. I asked her to think about her experience taking Filipina/x/o American Studies and why she thought the school board should adopt a resolution to support Ethnic studies. Reflecting on my prompt, she began writing down notes. The board meeting began, and school community members started lining up around the perimeter of the room to claim their space to share their thoughts with the school board during public comment. When it was her turn, she stood up at the podium microphone and shared:

Ethnic studies really help me understand the importance of community and how working together . . . helps continue the legacy of people who came before me and ***ensures that I share a spot on the same historical timeline*** *as everyone else.*

Ethnic studies will cure us from historical amnesia and also identify goals and the steps that we need to address oppression. I'm lucky enough to have experienced Ethnic studies through this elective. It's about time that students from here on out get the same experience.

After public comment, the school board voted unanimously to support the growth of Ethnic studies in the district.

This kuwento describing the advocacy of Jocyl's former Pinay student demonstrates the impact that learning counternarratives can have on student leaders. Because she had the opportunity to take Filipina/x/o American Studies in high school, she could identify that her story, as well as the story of her community, should be included "on the same historical timeline" as others in the world. Recognizing the need for counterstories, or kuwentos, in the high school history classroom led to her up-and-coming role as an agent of change in her community. She and other students who spoke at the podium that night saw themselves as people who could make and/or change history.

Kuwentos and kuwentuhan can be utilized as pedagogy and praxis, especially with Pinxy students in history education. On a broader scope, kuwentos and kuwentuhan call for people to understand the nuances in both as embodied practices that allow for one to make meaning of themselves and with others. When we engage in kuwentos and kuwentuhan, we embody the counternarratives that have been and are often omitted and misrepresented in education—these Filipina/x/o cultural practices allow us to historicize who we are, where we come from, and how we resist the dominant narratives that try to erase us. Kuwentos and kuwentuhan teach us that we deserve "a spot on the same historical timeline as everyone else."

CHAPTER 8

Testimonio as Healing Praxis in History Classrooms

M. YIANELLA BLANCO

Maya Chinchilla is a Guatemalan American poet known for her chapbook, *The Cha Cha Files: A Chapina Poética*, in which she describes her experiences as a Guatemalan woman living in the diaspora.[1] In her poem, "Maya Like the People," she closes with "tough stuff sweetheart big dreamer, corny tamale palabrista, calling on the silence and making it out" as a reference to herself as a Central American whose work highlights the contradictions of being a Central American in the US and how her work aims to uplift the histories and experiences of her community, despite decades of silence.[2] Her poetry serves as a powerful example of Central American testimonio and draws from a rich legacy of Central American testimonistas, freedom fighters, truth-tellers, agitators, and revolutionaries.[3] "Maya Like the People" illustrates the impact of testimonio by providing contesting narratives that trouble previous perceptions about Central America(ns). Chinchilla's poetry, like that of the many testimonios of other Central Americans, alters conversations about the richness and complexity of our histories and experiences, which are rarely included in PK–12 curricula. Though Central Americans now make up the third largest Latinx demographic in the United States, little is taught about us, and when it is, it is often done in ways that perpetuate stereotypical narratives of war, poverty, and violence. Testimonios are not only an opportunity to tell these histories and experiences from the perspective of Central Americans themselves, but they also contribute important alternative representations of the Central American experience, which are desperately needed in history classrooms.

CONTEXT

Oral traditions are deeply rooted in Latin American, Indigenous, and emancipatory struggles.[4] They have often been used as an avenue to expose brutality, disrupt silencing, and build solidarity among People of Color.[5] Testimonio, a revolutionary genre within these oral traditions, has been used by individuals to challenge dominant narratives by "situating the individual in communion with a collective experience marked by marginalization, oppression, or resistance."[6] The end result is the disruption of pervasive narratives that frame communities, particularly those who have been historically marginalized, by what they lack rather than what they have gained, what they bring, and how they continue to resist neocolonial and white supremacist power structures. Testimonios also provide critical contextualization for historical events and phenomena not typically challenged in history classrooms, such as those that uplift narratives of American "progress" or "meritocracy."

Testimonio differs from traditional oral history practices, memoirs, or autobiographies because it positions itself as urgent and is intentionally political. Testimonio rejects notions of neutrality or objectivity. It involves a critical reflection of personal experience within larger sociopolitical realities by engaging with Latin American social movements like Freire's process of conscientização. There is an explicit focus on achieving an in-depth understanding of the world, where "oppressed communities construct self-reflective movements to mobilize through critical pedagogies of empowerment and praxis."[7] The testimonistas reassume their agency by engaging a shared knowledge of oppression to resist and humanize their experiences. Further, testimonios are not simply shared orally. Part of the power of testimonio lies in the diversity of its medium. They can and have taken many forms, including dance, music, or even textiles.

While typically thought of as a "product," a narrative that one can read, watch, or listen to, testimonio is as much about the process as it is about the result. It is equally about the act of telling and listening. It represents what Cherríe Moraga termed theory in the flesh in that it is a way of inscribing struggles and understandings, creating new knowledge, and affirming our epistemologies in physical ways. With testimonio, we can "hear and read each other's stories through voices, silences, bodies, and emotions, through the goal of achieving new conocimientos, or understandings."[8] Engaging with testimonios is a means to elevate silences, represent the "other," reclaim authority to the narrative, and disentangle questions surrounding "legitimate" truths. Unlike conventional forms of historical inquiry, testimonio offers the possibility that multiple truths can coexist.

APPROACH TO THE PAST: CENTRAL AMERICAN TESTIMONIO

By emphasizing the process, especially one which is socially embedded and contextualized, testimonios challenge the history discipline's tendency to elevate texts as unbiased and objective products. Instead, testimonios move away from Eurocentric historical practices by positioning historical inquiry as not only something people do, experience, and share but also something that actively challenges the very definition of what "counts" as history and who decides. It is an agentic shift whereby testimonistas, often people who are not deemed as "experts," interject not only to challenge and contextualize dominant historical narratives but shift how historical events are recorded, shared, and legitimized.

Testimonios have also been instrumental in movement building and have been used to build cross-racial and ethnic solidarity. By listening to and telling of transcending struggles, hopes, pains, and dreams, an interdependent solidarity is formed akin to the Mayan philosophy *in lak'ech*, "Tu eres mi otro yo" or "You are my other me." The resulting interdependent solidarity connects people, such as educators and their students and families, across social positions, differences, languages, space, and time.[9] By listening to the story of one, we learn about the experiences of many.

Lastly and importantly, testimonio is an example of the role cultural practices can have in the process of healing. Testimonio can help "transcend pain toward a space for healing and societal transformation."[10] They provide opportunities for the testimonista and the listeners to be, know, and relate to one another in ways that are shaped by historical and contemporary social, political, and economic circumstances. Since cultural practices, like testimonios, are passed down intergenerationally, they often carry with them important lessons about identity and "anchor" who we are.

Healing-centered practices extend beyond healing as something that occurs strictly through the lens of clinical health and instead embraces a holistic view of well-being, including culturally grounded rituals and activities. Scholars of healing-centered pedagogical practices contend that young people's well-being and posttraumatic experiences benefit from culturally grounded practices to anchor them in a "solid sense of meaning, self-perception and purpose."[11] Since healing is experienced *collectively*, Shawn Ginwright argues, engaging young people in shared practices related to race, gender, ethnicity, or sexual orientation helps to build a healthy identity and sense of belonging. Previous examples of such practices include healing circles within Indigenous cultures or drumming circles rooted in African cultural principles. This chapter builds on this research by examining the healing potential of Central American testimonios when used with Central American youth.

IMPLICATIONS FOR PRACTICE

Testimonio as Healing Inspiration and Praxis for Educators and Students

> One of the most vital ways we sustain ourselves is by building communities of resistance, places where we know we are not alone.
>
> —bell hooks[12]

This chapter was born out of a research project in which six other Central American educators and I came together to dream and build curricula centered around Central American histories and experiences through testimonio. Table 8.1 outlines details about each of our cocreators. However, what the table does not capture is what brought us together, which were in equal parts our similarities and our differences. For example, we all identify as Central Americans, we are all either

TABLE 8.1 Central American collective cocreators

Cocreator	*State(s) taught*	*Subject area*	*Grade level*
Santiago	Georgia	English, Ethnic Studies	All grades
Sebastían	New York	Art	All grades
Miguel	California	US History, Ethnic Studies	Secondary
Blanca	Massachusetts	English as a Second Language	Elementary
Ziglilly	California	AP Spanish, Spanish I	Secondary
Roque	Virginia	English	Secondary

children of immigrants or are immigrants ourselves, and we are all educators. Our differences, however, played an equally important role in our collaboration. Though we were all educators, there was a range of teaching experiences, from being a first-year teacher to having fifteen-plus years of experience. Our grade level expertise ranged from elementary through high school, and even our subject matter varied. Initially, I hoped to recruit and work with social studies teachers specifically. Ultimately, however, we ended up with a mixed-subject group. Though not all of us taught social studies or history explicitly, we did all bring Central American histories and experiences into our classrooms.

As a collective, we met several times over the course of six months with two overarching goals: (1) to build community with other Central American educators by learning more about each other and ourselves, what brought us to teaching, and what sustains us in this work (2) to imagine and build classroom spaces about, for, and by Central Americans. We approached these goals in various ways, such as creating and sharing our own testimonios, which were filled with familial stories of immigration, displacement, and, at times, xenophobia and racism. We also selected a text to read together as a group. We chose *Solito, Solita: Crossing Borders with Youth Refugees from Central America*, a compilation of testimonios shared by Central American migrant youth, as our core text.[13] We chose this text because there is a wide variety of testimonios by Central Americans from which educators can choose to use in their own classrooms.[14] We read *Solito, Solita* independently and then reconvened together to discuss the curricular and pedagogical possibilities that surfaced from our shared reading, reflections, and discussions.

What emerged were not only our ideas around the use of testimonios within *Solito, Solita* but the creation and sharing of our own testimonios as Central American educators who identify as either immigrants or first-generation immigrants. There was also a power in doing this work as a collective—in reading the testimonios together, sharing our own, listening to each other, and using all of these to co-construct our understanding of Central American migration in the second half of the twenty-first century. This pedagogical model changed the power dynamics of learning history by positioning everyone in the group as someone with knowledge to share. This contrasts with traditional forms of learning history whereby knowledge is shared by reading decontextualized primary sources, which were pre-selected by an "expert" historian based on their tools of objectivity. Here, instead, we understand historical thinking and inquiry as one that is socially embedded and part of a social process. We learn about and construct a historical narrative as opposed to having one given to us.

After months of meeting, platicando,[15] sharing and listening to each other's testimonios, and reading those within our anchor text *Solito, Solita: Crossing Borders with Youth Refugees from Central America*, my six collaborators and I met one last time to share final reflections about the research process. Holding space for sharing not only closed out the research process in ways that honored our new relationships, our work together, and our individual growth, but it was also an opportunity for continued re/un/learnings and new theorizations of our lives as Central American educators teaching and learning about our own communities. A final affirmation that we had valuable knowledge and experiences to share.

To begin our final reflections, I offered the group a prompt, "If you had to summarize our experience together using one word, what word would you use and why?" I began by sharing my own word, which was "vulnerability," or "radical vulnerability," to be exact. Here, I drew from adrienne maree brown's definition of the phrase where she states being vulnerable becomes "another radical front—to feel your life, to be honest with your feelings, to offer to each other the trust of where we hurt and what we long for and what brings us joy."[16] I explained how this process forced me to further reckon with my purpose behind this work, my positionality, and the limitations therein, even as a Central American myself. I also shared that this space made me feel safe to do so. Though we had only just met a few months prior, I already felt a kinship between us that allowed me to be honest and vulnerable about my experiences in a way I had not in other spaces, including those with other teachers. My cocreators shared some of their final reflections as well:

> *I have felt really empowered here. There's a commitment here from everyone I have met, to make sure that we really do good for ourselves, and we do good for the people that come after us. There's this inherent goodness that I feel is emanating from this conversation, from this space and I'm leaving it feeling empowered.—Sebastián*
>
> *This process has made me reflective. It made me really think about why I'm teaching because everyone else here, I saw so much energy and so much enthusiasm, so much care for students. Y'all are so active and politically engaged and I look at all that and think, "whoa, this is so impressive and motivating." These are the teachers I love to be around. This is the supportive system we need to stay in this.—Miguel*
>
> *This process has felt humanizing. We all came into this space with different experiences, but we were allowed to be our full, authentic selves. We aren't perfect or*

experts, but we allowed ourselves to learn and grow. It was an example of what it means to feel seen, wholly and without judgment.—Roque

After sharing our final thoughts, we sat in silence, soaking up and sitting with each of the words offered in the space. Despite living in different parts of the country, and never sharing a physical space because our entire project took place via Zoom due to the ongoing pandemic, the opportunity to share, listen, dream, and build with each other led to feelings of growth, humanization, empowerment, reflection, and appreciation. It demonstrated how testimonio, in addition to providing a critical and culturally sustaining curriculum for young people, also served as a powerful process for teachers themselves. Below, I highlight how the process of sharing, listening, and reading testimonios affected how my cocreators in this research collective approached their work as history teachers. How this process helped us imagine a future in which classrooms could be spaces for healing with the use of testimonios.

Healing Through Affirmation of Knowledges

Our time together reaffirms the value of adding testimonios to history curriculum in several ways. To begin with, they reorient the ways in which Central America(ns) is/are often depicted in history classrooms. For example, rather than focusing exclusively on the horrors of the civil war in El Salvador, testimonios from people who experienced the war provide examples of resistance in the face of US-backed military intervention. One of the most well-known examples of Central American testimonio that could be brought into the classroom is *I, Rigoberta Menchú* by Ki'che' activist Rigoberta Menchú Tum. In her testimonio, she detailed the human rights violations committed by the Guatemalan Army during the country's civil war during the second half of the twenty-first century. Her personal account during the war helped raise invaluable awareness around the experiences of Indigenous people in Guatemala both before and during the war. Importantly, it also started crucial conversations regarding Indigenous rights and sovereignty in Central America and beyond that continue to this day.

Another well-known Central American testimonista who could provide a new historical perspective is Giaconda Belli, a Nicaraguan poet. Her writing explores her experiences fighting on behalf of the Sandinistas during the Nicaraguan revolution in the 1980s.[17] It sheds light on her experiences as a woman during the revolution and could be utilized in a unit on the Cold War and the Iran-Contra scandal, a topic most US history classes already include in their curriculum. Not only does she provide a gendered perspective, which history curricula frequently omit, but her memoir also details her day-to-day experiences living in Nicaragua before and during the war. Lessons on the Iran-Contra scandal typically center the roles of the United States and Iran, but a greater focus on Nicaragua could help students better understand how the United States has frequently intervened in Central America and caused political and social disruptions whose effects are still felt today.

The youth testimonios included in more recently published books, such as *Solito, Solita: Crossing Borders with Youth Refugees from Central America* focus less on the political unrest of their parents' generation and more on the social and economic impact war and other circumstances have had on their present lives. All the testimonistas within the book made the difficult decision to leave their homes and attempt to start anew in Mexico, the United States, or Canada. Their testimonios not only shift previous and current conceptions of Central America(ns) and migration, but they also offer new ones. In our work together, my cocreators and I drew from the brilliance and strength present within the testimonios to create new lessons focused on all they had to offer. Doing so, we reasoned, would provide opportunities for healing via giving students the ability to reconnect with the cultural practice of engaging with testimonios, as well as giving them a chance to learn about their own histories and experiences that were positive, highlighting their community's strength and resistance.

Healing Through Humanizing Portrayals

In addition to using testimonios to teach from and by Central Americans, my cocreators and I discussed how they advance our goal of creating a more humanizing history curriculum for Central Americans. Our emphasis on "humanizing" stems from Freire's work on humanizing pedagogy. In *Pedagogy of the Oppressed*, he describes it as a revolutionary approach to instruction that "ceases to be an instrument by which teachers can manipulate students, but rather expresses the consciousness of the students themselves."[18] Teachers who enact humanizing pedagogy cultivate problem-posing education where students are coinvestigators in dialogue with their teachers to develop mutual "conscientização" or critical consciousness.[19] Humanizing pedagogy includes a commitment to social change and to fighting against social injustice.

For example, one of our cocreators, Santiago elaborated on the potential testimonios have in providing "humanizing" curricula. He shared:

> What I appreciate most about the testimonios is that they provide a humanizing, bottom-up account of these events. First-person narratives enrich the historical record in ways that go beyond just the "data," the statistics on who was coming, from where, when, and how. Their stories give depth and meaning to those numbers. They might give us insight into their decision-making process, what they encountered and how they've persevered. They could also challenge stereotypes about our homelands. El Salvador is so "dangerous" right? But why is that? And is that all it is? I think it's important to have those perspectives because they give us an opportunity to interrogate the structural conditions behind migration too, like why we are in this mess in the first place.

In the spirit of Freire's humanizing pedagogy, Santiago uses testimonios to inspire learning that "perceives social, political, and economic contradictions . . . to take action against the oppressive elements of reality."[20] His use of testimonio drives students to ask important questions about who is migrating and why. His instruction would foster discussions that challenge stereotypes about the isthmus and this stereotype about it being only "dangerous." Testimonios offer opportunities to see the region as a place that also contains richness, rather than just violence, and in doing so, provide a direct challenge to dominant narratives around the region and the people who are from there.

Separately, Santiago explained how he would explicitly use the testimonios within his classroom to engage in more complex discussions around migration:

> I really liked this teaching strategy from Dr. Goldy Muhammad. She talks about "layering texts" where you use multiple texts to discuss a single topic. I could see myself using these testimonios and layering them with a video text that gives background about US intervention or exploitation. I would also bring in poetry from migrants themselves, and some graphs or statistics that show the big impact such wars have had on Central American displacement. The combination of different sources can illustrate the different angles of the issue in a way that really supports each other in presenting a comprehensive account of the conditions that force people to migrate.

In this example, Santiago folds youth testimonio into an existing pedagogical vision and set of practices vis-á-vis Dr. Muhammad's text layering strategy. Muhammad describes this strategy as a practice where "educators [use] multiple powerful and multimodal texts . . . to rouse new thought and be intellectually compelling in relation to critical issues and concepts that invite students' social critique and understanding of the local and global world."[21] The emphasis on "critical issues" and "social critique of the local and global world" is key in Santiago's vision of his use of testimonios. In his imagining, they serve a clear purpose: an opportunity for young people to challenge the conditions that force migration.

Alignment with Standards and Frameworks: It's Not Either/Or—It's Both/And

The examples of curricular possibilities with testimonio shared above demonstrate how, though testimonios are rarely seen in history curricula, it is not because they would be difficult to incorporate. The variety of perspectives, depth, and nuance of experiences afforded by testimonios make them a natural fit for common core standards and/or the C3 Framework. The C3 Framework, whose guiding principles "have direct and explicit connections to the Common Core State Standards," states that historical thinking requires "going beyond simply asking, 'What happened when?' to evaluating why and how events occurred and developments unfolded. It involves locating and assessing historical sources of many different types to understand the contexts of given historical eras and the perspectives of different individuals and groups within geographic units that range from the local to the global."[22] Testimonios add to the "many different types" of historical sources to "understand the contexts of given historical eras." In this way, the content within the testimonios is important, but so is the medium. By including testimonios, culturally grounded within Latinx and Indigenous cultures, we disrupt what is commonly seen as "academic" or "rigorous" texts. The uplifting and centering of testimonios in our classrooms signal to students that not only do our histories, but the way we share and pass down those histories, matter. We carry with us legitimate sources of knowledge that are worthy of study.

Further, testimonio augments and extends traditional understandings of historical thinking skills. Scholars of historical thinking have emphasized the importance of students practicing the skills of trained historians, such as sourcing, contextualizing, and corroboration in the classroom.[23] The inclusion of testimonios encourages students to practice exactly these skills. The examples from my cocreators illustrate how testimonios complicate what are often one-dimensional historical inquiries about immigration or about Latinx communities.[24] As Santiago pointed out, testimonios are significant in that they challenge students to look at the "how" and "why" of immigration. It is not enough to discuss the presence of immigrants in the United States; students ought to also have discussions about how and why we are here and what our experiences here are. Indeed, students cannot understand the so-called migrant crisis at the southern US border without also learning the history of US intervention and exploitation in Latin America throughout the nineteenth and twentieth centuries.[25] In other words, testimonios can help students contextualize historical events and phenomena.

To use another example highlighted above, if students were tasked with reading an excerpt from *I, Rigoberta Menchú* in a unit on the Cold War, students could be prompted to ask who Rigoberta Menchú is, when and where she lived, the sociopolitical context of her writing, and how these factors may have contributed to not only her writing but the impact of it. Reading the experiences of an Indigenous woman during and after the Guatemalan civil war, a war that was aided by American intervention in the region, is one way to contextualize the very real effects of American foreign policy.

Beyond historical thinking skills, testimonios intentionally encourage students to consider questions of power, injustice, resistance, and solidarity. Our testimonios and those within *Solito, Solita* forefronts issues of colonialism, racism, and xenophobia in conversations about American foreign policy and migration. In this way, incorporating testimonios within history classrooms represent the "liminal space of possibility" called upon by scholars who seek to bridge historical thinking skills and critical scholarship.[26] As Maribel Santiago and Tadashi Dozono argue, history education scholars often feel limited by a false dichotomy between historical thinking skills and research that centers on histories of marginalization and confronts systems of power and injustice. Teachers, too, often feel as if they must choose one approach over the other. Clint Smith reminds us that we "do not have to choose between a rigorous lesson and a culturally responsive one. Our current political moment, and indeed our nation's history, demands both."[27] Testimonios are but one way in which we can achieve both and beyond.

CLOSING THOUGHTS

Solito, Solita begins with a forward from Javier Zamora, a Salvadoran American poet who migrated unaccompanied to the United States at nine years old to reunite with his parents, both of whom left El Salvador as a result of the US-backed civil war. In his forward, he posits that "we share ourselves, our lives, I think, in the hopes that we can turn this other self into a physical thing—a recording, a story, a book, art—so that we can better control it, so we can see it, mold it, and hopefully understand that we can and should treat ourselves better."[28] Testimonios, both process and product, routinely act as restoration, a form of healing from trauma. They can be a powerful teaching tool for educators who seek to uplift their Central American youth and affirm that their stories carry wisdom. As Santiago mentioned during one of our pláticas, "testimonios can teach us to be kinder and better to ourselves."

Zamora later refers to his trauma as his "creation myth" because myths change, and though myths are often at one point true, they "shouldn't be truth forever."[29] Here, Zamora, like my cocreators, is asserting that our stories are not just of trauma but also of moments of joy, love, and laughter that should not be forgotten and for which we can "envision a better future."[30] Testimonios allow us to see Central America(ns) as more than suffering. Instead, we are made up of the softer and nourishing, as well as the harder and more resilient materials of the earth. We should honor that through a practice of joy, love, and laughter in the classroom and our daily lives. We, as a research collective and curriculum dreaming team, are still learning how to do that, but the inclusion of testimonios in our history curriculum feels like an entryway to manifesting it. We continue to look forward to the ways that the creation myths of Central America(ns) may temporarily wound us but also build us up again with a greater understanding of ourselves, each other, and our world.

Afterword: Shifting Paradigms in History Education Through the Mind, Body, and Heart

What were your history classes like growing up? How have your own experiences in history education informed your current approaches to thinking, teaching, and learning about history—and to your reading and understanding of the purpose and chapters in this book?

These were the questions that lived rent free in my mind, body, and heart as I journeyed through the chapters of this book. I found myself wishing that my own history classes growing up mirrored the approaches in this text and that I would've had more books like this to support my early development and growth as a history and Ethnic studies educator.

Until eleventh grade, none of my history classes reflected my lived experiences or ancestry. In the rare instances when people who looked like me were included in the curriculum, their stories were filtered through the lens of whiteness. Taking Ethnic studies during my junior year of high school was the first time in my life that I learned a history in which I could place myself and my ancestors. Learning a history that contextualized the structural realities of my community affirmed my humanity, my feelings, and my lived experiences as a multiracial Woman of Color. This transformative and healing experience provided a visceral lesson in the difference between being included and being centered and has anchored my work in history and Ethnic studies education for over twenty years—as a middle and high school history and Ethnic studies teacher, school leader, professor, and teacher educator.

The importance of centering, rather than simply including, the narratives, lived experiences, worldviews, ways of knowing, and humanity of those who have been silenced by what Michel-Rolph Trouillot refers to as the "power and production of history" is a central theme across the chapters in this book, with each chapter offering approaches to the teaching of history that honor the complex and nuanced realities of racialized peoples and communities.[1]

I often incorporate "mind, body, heart" check-ins and journaling into the courses that I teach as a way to genuinely gauge how my students are entering the space and remind everyone that the study of our collective past and present is more than a cognitive exercise; it's an embodied one. In that spirit, I invite you to check in with your mind, body, and heart through the following questions:

MIND: What are some things you've learned and unlearned about history and history education while reading this book? How do your history and the history of your ancestors connect with the histories shared by the contributing authors?

BODY: What came up in your body as you read through the different racial/ethnic community approaches to history and history education? When did you experience visceral reactions to the text? When did your muscles constrict or relax while reading?

HEART: What types of emotions did you experience while reading? How did each of the chapters make you feel? In what ways did your emotions support or impede your ability to consider the curricular and pedagogical possibilities offered by the various authors in this book?

How do your responses to these questions and your reading of this book compel you to *think, speak, listen, and act*?

In the introduction to one of the core texts that I assign in several of my courses, "My Grandmother's Hands: Racialized Trauma and the Pathway to Mending Our Hearts and Bodies," Resmaa Menakem writes:

> For the past three decades, we've earnestly tried to address white-body supremacy in America with reason, principles, and ideas—using dialogue, forums, discussions, education, and mental training but we've focused our efforts in the

> wrong directions. We've tried to teach our brains to think better about race. But white-body supremacy doesn't live in our thinking brains. It lives and breathes in our bodies.[2]

Consider Menakem's words in relation to your mind, body, heart reflection and to the title and purpose of this book, *Shifting the Lens in History Education: Centering Racial and Ethnic Knowledge in the Classroom*. In their introduction, Maribel Santiago and Tadashi Dozono explicitly share the trauma, pain, and healing they experienced in their journey of writing and editing this book and the personal and professional consequences of conforming to Eurocentric norms that intellectualize the collective human suffering of racialized and colonized peoples in history education. They state, "In reducing history to the mastering of skills, history is framed more as an individual cognitive act," and call upon educators to change how they think about and practice history education. This epistemological and pedagogical shift must begin with an honest and rigorous interrogation of ourselves, of our dominant and counter sources of knowledge, and a commitment to embracing the cognitive and affective dimensions inherent to a history education that is rooted in our communities, the communities of our students, and communities that we cocreate with our students when we study the past, rather than a history education that treats racialized peoples as optional objects of historical inquiry.

SHIFTING CURRICULUM AND PEDAGOGY TO CENTER RACIAL AND ETHNIC COMMUNITY APPROACHES TO HISTORY IN SCHOOLS

How do you currently teach and talk about race and ethnicity in your classroom? How is race/ethnicity addressed in your curriculum and pedagogy? What curricular and pedagogical shifts do you feel compelled to make after reading this book and why?

One of the key aims of this book is a call for history educators to "shift from a focus on isolated skills to process" and to honor the ways that "history does something with community." Shifting one's pedagogy and curriculum to center the racial and ethnic community approaches in this book first requires what Shawn Ginwright refers to as a "shift in thinking from *technical pedagogy*, which focuses on what teachers should know and what teachers should do, to *relational pedagogy*, which focuses on who teachers should be, and on removing the psycho-spiritual obstacles that prevent teachers from establishing quality relationships with young people."[3] Connecting the learning in classrooms with the lived experiences of students in responsible and meaningful ways requires knowing who your students are and co-constructing a classroom community that makes space for students' emotions, as well as your own.

Each of the approaches in this book is rooted in sacred practices and ways of knowing and being and must be treated with dignity, respect, and care. I was deeply moved by each author's personal relationship with the approaches that they've developed with and in community and appreciated each moment that challenged me to examine my own proximity and distance to the material. I also want to appreciate and uplift the explicit cautions and guidelines outlined by the authors as important reminders to honestly assess one's readiness to bring any of these practices into the classroom.

I encourage readers to revisit each of the racial/ethnic community approaches and to explore the following questions through the mind, body, and heart: *What does each chapter reveal about your current approaches to history education? How did certain chapters illuminate gaps in your curricular and pedagogical approaches? Which approaches felt familiar or incongruent with what you already do in your classroom? Which approaches reminded you of former or current students? Where did you experience connection and resonance? How might your previous understanding, if any, of the culturally rich histories that each of these approaches come from influence how you might take up these ideas and approaches in your own classroom?*

With the history and Ethnic studies teachers and graduate students that I currently work with in mind and heart, I offer some additional curricular and pedagogical considerations and possibilities for each chapter and invite readers and educators to revisit each chapter and frame your own questions for further reflection and inquiry.

Chapter 1: The Legacy of Racial and Ethnic Community-Led Education:
What are the legacies of racial and ethnic community-led education in your surrounding communities?
In what ways does your current curriculum and pedagogy affirm or deny the lived experiences of your students and their ancestors as racialized beings?
Whose voices, lives, histories, and experiences are centered, celebrated, condemned, or silenced in your curriculum?

Chapter 2: Queer of Color Horizons: Reorienting History Education Through Queer of Color Methods:

How can incorporating students' and/or historical protagonists' queer and racialized identities into your teaching of history challenge Eurocentric approaches and methods?

How might you engage students' funds of disorientation and alienation as productive entry points to historical inquiry?

How can you incorporate more archival content that engages the strange, weird, alien, silenced, and misunderstood into your curriculum?

Chapter 3: Expecting Indigenous Presence: Indigenous Pasts, Presents, and Futures in K–12 Social Studies:

How have you educated or how can you educate yourself about contemporary Indigenous issues, and how will you share your learning with students?

Which resources provided throughout this chapter can be incorporated into your current curriculum and practice? Which resources require additional study before you incorporate them into your classroom?

How will you weave contemporary Indigenous voices and issues into your curriculum and classroom using materials that Native people have chosen to create and curate for others?

Chapter 4: We Have Joy but What About Rage? An Examination of Race and Emotions:

How do you currently invite and engage the spectrum of emotions with your students as they study the past?

Where do Black rage and Black joy currently live and breathe in your curriculum?

How might you apply the CARE framework to any of your current units of study?

Chapter 5: "Remediando" Latinx Blackness: AfroIndigenous Spiritual Practice as History Pedagogy:

Where do spirituality and/or spiritual practices currently live in your study of the past?

How do/might you center AfroIndigenous and AfroLatinx histories and practices as history pedagogy?

How might incorporating AfroIndigenous and AfroLatinx historical narratives and practice disrupt enactments of anti-Blackness in history education?

Chapter 6: Embracing Palestinian Oral Histories and Narratives in History Education:

How do you currently engage oral histories and storytelling to challenge and/or expand the limits of written archival materials in your curriculum?

How might you center Palestinian (her)storytelling in your curriculum to amplify Palestinian narratives in the face of the ongoing genocide and historical silencing?

How might you incorporate the narratives and accounts of Palestinian journalists like Bisan Owda and Lama Jamous into your curriculum and into lessons on how history is documented and chronicled?

Chapter 7: Centering Pinxy Narratives: Kuwentos and Kuwentuhan in History Education:

How might you offer each of your students "a spot on the same historical timeline as everyone else"?

How do you honor student agency in defining historical ideas and concepts in your classroom?

How do/might you center the lives and narratives of your students and their families as historically significant sources of knowledge and learning?

Chapter 8: Testimonio as Healing Praxis in History Classrooms:

How do you model and exercise vulnerability with your students?

When and how do you allow your full humanity to show up in how historical inquiry is practiced in your classroom?

Where can you incorporate testimonios into your curriculum? How might incorporating testimonios into your curriculum shift the questions and discussions in your classroom?

BUILDING A BEAUTIFUL FUTURE THROUGH OUR STUDY OF THE PAST

I hope that these questions can serve as reminders, affirmations, and/or guides as we take up Santiago and Dozono's call to rupture dominant approaches in history education that are rooted in Eurocentric epistemologies and frameworks. A history education that heals requires more than a focus on cultivating students' skills in historical inquiry and practice; it requires a paradigmatic shift toward the racial and ethnic community approaches in this book in the study of our collective pasts to more fully contextualize our present as we work to co-construct a future that embraces our complexity and emotionality as racialized, storied beings. May we all continue to grow in our abilities to teach, learn, and engage in histories that actively interrupt curricular and pedagogical enactments of oppression and that humanize our students, ourselves, and our ancestors.

Christina Villareal, PhD
Lecturer on Education
Harvard Graduate School of Education

Notes

Foreword

1. Thomas King, *The Truth About Stories: A Native Narrative* (University of Minnesota Press, 2008), 2.
2. Saidiya Hartman, "Venus in Two Acts," *Small Axe: A Caribbean Journal of Criticism* 12, no. 2 (2008): 1–14.
3. Yoon K. Pak, Latasha Louise Nesbitt, and Suzanne M. Reilly, eds., *Extraordinary Lives of Ordinary People: Oral Histories of (Mis)Educational Opportunities in Challenging Notions of Achievement* (n.p.: Common Ground Publishing, 2018), 11.
4. Gabriel Rodriguez, "Understanding Latina/o Identity and Community in a White and Well-Resourced Chicagoland Suburban High School" (PhD diss., University of Illinois at Urbana-Champaign, 2018).
5. Mirelsie Velázquez, "Lessons from the Past: Listening to Our Stories, Reading Our Lives: The Place of Oral Histories in Our Lives," in *Handbook of Historical Studies in Education: Debates, Tensions, and Directions*, ed. Tanya Fitzgerald (n.p.: Springer, 2019), 863–75.
6. An Act, H.B. 1775, Oklahoma State Legislature (2021), http://webserver1.lsb.state.ok.us/cf_pdf/2021-22%20ENR/hB/HB1775%20ENR.PDF.
7. Angie Morrill and Eve Tuck, "Before Dispossession, or Surviving It," *Liminalities: A Journal of Performance Studies* 12, no. 1 (2016).
8. Mirelsie Velázquez, "De donde tu eres: Pedagogies of a Puerto Rican Academic," in *College Curriculum at the Crossroads: Women of Color Reflect and Resist*, ed. Kirsten T. Edwards and Maria del Guadalupe Davidson (Routledge, 2017), 137–47.
9. Yi-Fu Tuan, *Space and Place: The Perspective of Experience* (University of Minnesota Press, 2001 reprint).
10. Velázquez, "Family migration and educational trajectories" in *Extraordinary Lives of Ordinary People: Oral Histories of (Mis)Educational Opportunities in Challenging Notions of Achievement*, ed. Yoon K. Pak, Latasha Louise Nesbitt, and Suzanne M. Reilly (n.p.: Common Ground Publishing, 2018), 86.
11. Richard White, *Remembering Ahanagran: Storytelling in a Family's Past* (New York: Hill and Wang Press, 1998).
12. *El Archivo Project*, Puerto Rican Arts Alliance, https://www.praachicago.org/el-archivo-project.
13. Gloria Anzaldúa, *Borderlands/La Frontera: The New Mestiza* (San Francisco: Spinsters/Aunt Lute, 1987).

Introduction

1. Linda S. Levstik and Keith C. Barton, *Doing History: Investigating with Children in Elementary and Middle Schools* (New York: Routledge, 2022); Peter Seixas, "A Model of Historical Thinking," *Educational Philosophy and Theory* 49, no. 6 (2017): 593–605, https://doi.org/10.1080/00131857.2015.1101363; Sam Wineburg, *Historical Thinking and*

Other Unnatural Acts: Charting the Future of Teaching the Past (Philadelphia, PA: Temple University Press, 2001).

2. Ernst Breisach, *Historiography: Ancient, Medieval, and Modern* (Chicago, IL: University of Chicago Press, 2007); Georg G. Iggers, *Historiography in the Twentieth Century: From Scientific Objectivity to the Postmodern Challenge* (Middletown, CT: Wesleyan University Press, 1997); Peter Novick, *The Noble Dream: The "Objectivity Question" and the American Historical Profession* (Cambridge: Cambridge University Press, 1988).
3. Maribel Santiago and Tadashi Dozono, "History Is Critical: Addressing the False Dichotomy Between Historical Inquiry and Criticality," *Theory & Research in Social Education* 50, no. 2 (2022): 173–95, https://doi.org/10.1080/00933104.2022.2048426; Tadashi Dozono, "The Passive Voice of White Supremacy: Tracing Epistemic and Discursive Violence in World History Curriculum," *Review of Education, Pedagogy, and Cultural Studies* 42, no. 1 (2020): 1–26, https://doi.org/10.1080/10714413.2020.1721261.
4. Marjan de Groot-reuvekamp, Anje Ros, and Carla van Boxtel, "Improving Elementary School Students' Understanding of Historical Time: Effects of Teaching with 'Timewise,'" *Theory and Research in Social Education* 46, no. 1 (2018): 35–67, https://doi.org/10.1080/00933104.2017.1357058; Mark Smith, Joel Breakstone, and Sam Wineburg, "History Assessments of Thinking: A Validity Study," *Cognition and Instruction* 37, no. 1 (2019): 118–44, https://doi.org/10.1080/07370008.2018.1499646.
5. Cinthia Salinas, Brooke Blevins, and Caroline C. Sullivan, "Critical Historical Thinking: When Official Narratives Collide with 'Other' Narratives," *Multicultural Perspectives* 14, no. 1 (2012): 18–27.
6. Mari J. Matsuda, "When the First Quail Calls: Multiple Consciousness as Jurisprudential Method," in *Critical Race Theory: The Cutting Edge*, ed. R. Delgado and J. Stefancic (Philadelphia, PA: Temple University Press, 2013), 31–34.
7. Dolores Delgado Bernal, Rebeca Burciaga, and Judith Flores Carmona, "Chicana/Latina Testimonios: Mapping the Methodological, Pedagogical, and Political," *Equity & Excellence in Education* 45, no. 3 (2012): 1, https://doi.org/10.1080/10665684.2012.698149.

Chapter 1

1. Wayne J. Urban and Jennings L. Wagoner, *American Education: A History*, 5th ed. (New York" Routledge, 2013).
2. Urban and Wagoner, *American Education: A History.*
3. Urban and Wagoner, *American Education: A History.*
4. Michael B. Katz, *The Irony of Early School Reform: Educational Innovation in Mid-Nineteenth Century Massachusetts* (New York: Teachers College Press, 2001).
5. Urban and Wagoner, *American Education: A History.*
6. David B Tyack, *The One Best System: A History of American Urban Education* (Cambridge, MA: Harvard University Press, 1974).
7. Tyack, *The One Best System.*
8. Tyack, *The One Best System.*
9. Erika Lee, *America for Americans: A History of Xenophobia in the United States* (New York: Basic Books, 2019).
10. Tyack, *The One Best System.*
11. Tyack, *The One Best System*, 110.
12. Keith A. Mayes, *The Unteachables: Disability Rights and the Invention of Black Special Education* (Minneapolis: University of Minnesota Press, 2022); J. Blaine Hudson, "Scientific

Racism: The Politics of Tests, Race and Genetics," *The Black Scholar* 25, no. 1 (1995): 3–10; Urban and Wagoner, *American Education: A History.*

13. David Wallace Adams, *Education for Extinction: American Indians and the Boarding School Experience, 1875–1928* (Lawrence: University Press of Kansas, 1995).
14. ShaVonte' Mills, "An African School for African Americans: Black Demands for Education in Antebellum Boston," *History of Education Quarterly* 61, no. 4 (November 1, 2021): 478–502, https://doi.org/10.1017/heq.2021.38.
15. Mills, "An African School," 479–80.
16. Wilson J. Moses, *Classical Black Nationalism: From the American Revolution to Marcus Garvey* (New York: New York University Press, 1996).
17. Mills, "An African School."
18. Mills, "An African School."
19. Mills, "An African School," 480.
20. James D. Anderson, *The Education of Blacks in the South, 1860–1935* (Chapel Hill: University of North Carolina Press, 1988).
21. Leon F. Litwack, "The White Man's Fear of the Educated Negro: How the Negro Was Fitted for His Natural and Logical Calling," *Journal of Blacks in Higher Education*, no. 20 (Season 02 1998): 100–108, https://doi.org/10.2307/2999249, 91.
22. Litwack, "The White Man's Fear," 90.
23. Anderson, *The Education of Blacks in the South.*
24. Anderson, *The Education of Blacks in the South.*
25. Russell Rickford, *We Are an African People: Independent Education, Black Power, and the Radical Imagination* (Oxford: Oxford University Press, 2016).
26. Anne Galletta, "Under One Roof, through Many Doors: Understanding Racial Equality in an Unequal World" (PhD diss., City University of New York, 2003).
27. Rickford, *We Are an African People.*
28. Carlos Kevin Blanton, *The Strange Career of Bilingual Education in Texas, 1836–1981* (College Station: Texas A&M University Press, 2004).
29. Robert L. McCaul, *The Black Struggle for Public Schooling in Nineteenth-Century Illinois* (Carbondale: Southern Illinois University Press, 2009).
30. Sarah Catherine K. Moore, *A History of Bilingual Education in the US: Examining the Politics of Language Policymaking* (Blue Ridge Summit, PA: Multilingual Matters, 2021).
31. Blanton, *The Strange Career*; Moore, *A History of Bilingual Education.*
32. Aida Barrera, "The 'Little Schools' in Texas, 1897–1964: Educating Mexican American Children," *American Educational History Journal* 33, no. 2 (2006): 35–45.
33. Maribel Santiago, Cati V De Los Ríos, and Kris D Gutiérrez, "Historicizing Latinx Civic Agency and Contemporary Lived Civics," Report (National Academy of Education, 2021), https://naeducation.org/educating-for-civic-reasoning-and-discourse/.
34. Jovita González Mireles, *Life along the Border: A Landmark Tejana Thesis* (College Station: Texas A&M University Press, 2006).
35. Cinthia Salinas, "El Colegio Altamirano (1897–1958): New Histories of Chicano Education in the Southwest," *The Educational Forum* 65, no. 1 (2001): 80–86.
36. Mireles, *Life along the Border*, 113.
37. Salinas, "El Colegio Altamirano," 84.
38. Mario Rios Perez, *Subjects of Resistance: Education, Race, and Transnational Life in Mexican Chicago, 1910–1940.* (Rutgers University Press, Forthcoming).
39. Rios Perez, *Subjects of Resistance.*

40. Santiago, De Los Ríos, and Gutiérrez, "Historicizing Latinx Civic Agency."
41. Santiago, De Los Ríos, and Gutiérrez, "Historicizing Latinx Civic Agency," 210.
42. Juan Rulfo, *Altamirano: Vida, Tiempo, Obra* (Juan Pablo Editor, 2014).
43. Barrera, "The 'Little Schools in Texas," 38.
44. Rulfo, *Altamirano.*
45. Joyce J. Kuo, "Excluded, Segregated and Forgotten: A Historical View of the Discrimination of Chinese Americans in Public Schools," *Asian American Law Journal* 5, no. 1 (January 1998): 181–212, https://doi.org/10.15779/Z385G39.
46. Kuo, "Excluded, Segregated and Forgotten."
47. Kuo, "Excluded, Segregated and Forgotten," 193.
48. Shizhan Yuan, "Chinese Heritage Language Schools in the United States," in *Oxford Research Encyclopedia of Education*, 2023.
49. Yuan, "Chinese Heritage Language Schools in the United States," 2.
50. Kacie Y. Manabe, "Uncle Sam's Language School: How American Hegemony and Imperialism Altered Learning of Japanese and Hawaiian Language in Hawai'i," *Mānoa Horizons* 4 (2019): 1–9.
51. Noriko Shimada, "Wartime Dissolution and Revival of the Japanese Language Schools in Hawai'i: Persistence of Ethnic Culture," *Journal of Asian American Studies* 1, no. 2 (1998): 121–51, https://doi.org/10.1353/jaas.1998.0022.
52. Noriko Asato, "Religious Conflict among Hawaii Nikkei and How Japanese Entered the Public School Curriculum, 1896–1924," *Japanese Language and Literature* 42, no. 1 (April 2008): 63–94.
53. Noriko Asato, "Mandating Americanization: Japanese Language Schools and the Federal Survey of Education in Hawai'i, 1916–1920," *History of Education Quarterly* 43, no. 1 (2003): 10–38.
54. Asato, "Religious Conflict among Hawaii Nikkei."
55. Noriko Asato, *Teaching Mikadoism: The Attack on Japanese Language Schools in Hawaii, California, and Washington, 1919–1927* (Honolulu: University of Hawaii Press, 2005).
56. Asato, "Mandating Americanization."
57. Shimada, "Wartime Dissolution."
58. Adams, *Education for Extinction.*
59. Christina Snyder, "The Rise and Fall and Rise of Civilizations: Indian Intellectual Culture during the Removal Era," *Journal of American History* 104, no. 2 (September 2017): 386–409, https://doi.org/10.1093/jahist/jax175.
60. Snyder, "The Rise and Fall and Rise of Civilizations."
61. Snyder, "The Rise and Fall and Rise of Civilizations."
62. K. Tsianina Lomawaima and Teresa L. McCarty, *"To Remain an Indian": Lessons in Democracy from a Century of Native American Education* (New York: Teachers College Press, 2006).
63. Julie L. Davis, *Survival Schools: The American Indian Movement and Community Education in the Twin Cities* (Minneapolis: University of Minnesota Press, 2013).
64. Davis, *Survival Schools.*
65. Davis, *Survival Schools.*
66. Roxanne Dunbar-Ortiz, *An Indigenous Peoples' History of the United States* (Boston: Beacon Press, 2014).
67. Urban and Wagoner, *American Education: A History.*

Chapter 2

1. Judith Butler, *Gender Trouble: Feminism and the Subversion of Identity*, 2nd ed. (New York: Routledge Classics, 2006; first published in 1990).
2. David Lowenthal, *The Past is a Foreign Country* (New York: Cambridge University Press, 1985); James Wertsch, *Mind as Action* (New York: Oxford University Press, 1998); Hans-Georg Gadamer, *Truth and Method,* trans. Joel Weinsheimer and Donald G. Marshall (New York: Continuum, 2012; first published in 1960). For Lowenthal, the identity of the present encounters the past as a foreign country. For Wertsch and a Vygotsky lineage, this encounter is mediated action. For Gadamer, it is a fusion of horizons.
3. Sam Wineburg, *Historical Thinking and Other Unnatural Acts* (Philadelphia, PA: Temple University Press, 2001), 6.
4. Tadashi Dozono, *Discipline Problems: How Students of Color Trouble Whiteness in Schools* (Philadelphia: University of Pennsylvania Press), 130.
5. Tadashi Dozono, "Teaching Alternative and Indigenous Gender Systems in World History: A Queer Approach," *History Teacher* 50, no. 3 (2017): 425–47.
6. Roderick A. Ferguson, *Aberrations in Black: Toward a Queer of Color Critique* (Minneapolis: University of Minnesota Press, 2004), 26.
7. Maria Lugones, "Comment: It's All in Having a History," in *Gay Latino Studies: A Critical Reader*, ed. Michael Hames-García and Ernesto Javier Martínez (Durham, NC: Duke University Press, 2011), 51.
8. Lugones, "Comment," 50.
9. Michael Hames-García and Ernesto Javier Martínez, "Introduction," in *Gay Latino Studies: A Critical Reader*, ed. Michael Hames-García and Ernesto Javier Martínez (Durham, NC: Duke University Press, 2011), 4.
10. Tan Hoang Nguyen, *A View from the Bottom: Asian American Masculinity and Sexual Representation* (Durham, NC: Duke University Press, 2014).
11. Darieck Scott, *Extravagant Abjection: Blackness, Power, and Sexuality in the African American Literary Imagination* (New York: New York University Press, 2010).
12. Frantz Fanon, *Black Skin, White Masks,* trans. Richard Philcox (New York: Grove Press, 2008; first published 1952 by Editions du Seuil).
13. José Esteban Muñoz, *Disidentifications: Queers of Color and the Performance of Politics* (Minneapolis: University of Minnesota Press, 1999), 4.
14. Tadashi Dozono, "Queer Worlding as Historical Inquiry for Insurgent Freedom-Dreaming," in *Insurgent Social Studies: Scholar-Educators Disrupting Erasure & Marginality,* ed. Sarah B. Shear, Natasha H. Merchant, and Wayne Au (Gorham, ME: Myers Education Press, 2022).
15. José Esteban Muñoz, *Cruising Utopia: The Then and There of Queer Futurity* (New York: New York University Press, 2009), 1.
16. Muñoz, *Cruising Utopia*, 12.
17. Hans-Georg Gadamer, *Truth and Method,* trans. Joel Weinsheimer and Donald G. Marshall (New York: Continuum, 2012; first published 1960), 238.
18. Nadia Ellis, *Territories of the Soul: Queered Belonging in the Black Diaspora* (Durham: Duke University Press, 2015), 3.
19. Kadji Amin, *Disturbing Attachments: Genet, Modern Pederasty, and Queer History* (Durham, NC: Duke University Press, 2017), 10.
20. Amin, *Disturbing Attachments*, 11.

21. Christina Sharpe, *In the Wake: On Blackness and Being* (Durham, NC: Duke University Press, 2016). "I want to think of 'the wake' as a problem of and for thought. I want to think 'care' as a problem for thought. I want to think care in the wake as a problem for thinking and of and for Black non/being in the world" (5).
22. Sharpe, *In the Wake*, 7.
23. Wineburg, *Historical Thinking.*
24. Emma Perez, *The Decolonial Imaginary: Writing Chicanas into History* (Bloomington: Indiana University Press, 1999), xiii.
25. C. Riley Snorton, *Black on Both Sides: A Racial History of Trans Identity* (Minneapolis: University of Minnesota Press, 2017), 6.
26. Bruce A. VanSledright, "Fifth Graders Investigating History in the Classroom: Results from a Researcher-Practitioner Design Experiment," *Elementary School Journal* 103, no. 2 (2002): 131–60.
27. Snorton, *Black on Both Sides*, 8.
28. Snorton, *Black on Both Sides*, ix.
29. Anjali Arondekar, *For the Record: On Sexuality and the Colonial Archive in India* (Durham, NC: Duke University Press, 2009), 3.
30. Arondekar, *For the Record*, 1.
31. Saidiya Hartman, "Venus in Two Acts," *Small Axe* 12, no. 2 (2008): 11.
32. Hartman, "Venus in Two Acts," 12.
33. Perez, *The Decolonial Imaginary*, 27.
34. Dozono, "Queer Worlding."
35. See, for example, the science fiction writings of Octavia Butler and Samuel Delaney.

Chapter 3

1. Patrick Wolfe, "Settler Colonialism and the Elimination of the Native," *Journal of Genocide Research* 8, no. 4 (2006): 387–409.
2. Wayne Journell, "An Incomplete History: Representation of American Indians in State Social Studies Standards," *Journal of American Indian Education* 48, no. 2 (2009): 18–32; Christine Rogers Stanton, "The Curricular Indian Agent: Discursive Colonization and Indigenous (Dys)Agency in U.S. History Textbooks," *Curriculum Inquiry* 44, no. 5 (2014): 649–76; Sarah B. Shear, "Cultural Genocide Masked as Education: U.S. History Textbooks Coverage of Indigenous Education Policies," in *Doing Race in Social Studies: Critical Perspectives*, ed. Prentice T. Chandler (Charlotte: Information Age Publishing, 2015), 13–40; Sarah B. Shear, et al., "Manifesting Destiny: Re/Presentations of Indigenous Peoples in K–12 U.S. History Standards," *Theory and Research in Social Education* 43, no. 1 (2015): 68–101; Sarah B. Shear, Leilani Sabzalian, and Jimmy Snyder, "Rhetorics of Recognition and Erasure: Indigenous Citizenship and Sovereignty in U.S. Civics And Government Standards" (National Council for the Social Studies—College & University Faculty Assembly, Chicago, November 28, 2018).
3. Joyce E. King, "Dysconscious Racism: Ideology, Identity, and the Miseducation of Teachers," *Journal of Negro Education* 60, no. 2 (1991): 133–46, https://doi.org/10.2307/2295605; Cornel Pewewardy, Anna Lees, and Hyuny Clark-Shim, "The Transformational Indigenous Praxis Model: Stages for Developing Critical Consciousness in Indigenous Education," *Wicaso Sa Review* 33, no. 1 (2018): 38–69; Cornel Pewewardy, Anna Lees, and Robin Zape-tah-hol-ah Minthorn, *Unsettling Settler-Colonial Education: The Transformational Indigenous Praxis Model* (New York: Teachers College Press, 2022).

4. Meredith L. McCoy et al., "Restoring Indigenous Systems of Relationality" (Testimony, Center for Humans and Nature, October 7, 2020), https://www.humansandnature.org/restoring-indigenous-systems-of-relationality; Meixi et al., "When Learning Is Life Giving: Redesigning Schools With Indigenous Systems of Relationality," *AERA Open* 8 (January 1, 2022), https://doi.org/10.1177/23328584211062587; Leilani Sabzalian, "Curricular Standpoints and Native Feminist Theories: Why Native Feminist Theories Should Matter to Curriculum Studies," *Curriculum Inquiry* 48, no. 3 (May 27, 2018): 359–82, https://doi.org/10.1080/03626784.2018.1474710; Turtle Island Social Studies Collective, "Indigenous Futurities and the Responsibilities of Social Studies," in *Dreaming Out Loud: Critical Race Theory and Social Studies Futures*, ed. Amanda E. Vickery and Noreen Naseem Rodríguez (New York: Teachers College Press, 2022), 153–63.
5. Eve Tuck, "Suspending Damage: A Letter to Communities," *Harvard Educational Review* 79, no. 3 (2009): 409–27.
6. Leslie Locklear and Meredith L. McCoy, "Building Safe Spaces: Celebrating Teachers Who Support Native Youth," *Bit & Grain*, October 4, 2017, https://www.ednc.org/building-safe-spaces-celebrating-teachers-support-native-youth/; Meredith L. McCoy, Leilani Sabzalian, and Tommy Ender, "Alternative Strategies for Family History Projects: Rethinking Practice in Light of Indigenous Perspectives," *History Teacher* 54, no. 3 (2021): 473–501.
7. Ashley Cordes and Leilani Sabzalian, "The Urgent Need for Anticolonial Media Literacy," *International Journal of Multicultural Education* 22, no. 2 (2020): 182–201; Leilani Sabzalian, *Indigenous Children's Survivance in Public Schools* (New York: Routledge, 2019).
8. Turtle Island Social Studies Collective, "Beyond Pocahontas: Learning from Indigenous Women Changemakers," *Social Studies and the Young Learner* 31, no. 3 (2019): 7–13. For more on myths of replacement, see Jean O'Brien, *Firsting and Lasting: Writing Indians out of Existence in New England* (Minneapolis: University of Minnesota Press, 2010).
9. Gleb Raygorodetsky, "Indigenous Peoples Defend Earth's Biodiversity—But They're in Danger," *National Geographic*, November 16, 2018, https://www.nationalgeographic.com/environment/article/can-indigenous-land-stewardship-protect-biodiversity-.
10. McCoy et al., "Restoring Indigenous Systems of Relationality."
11. In addition to blogs like Nambé Pueblo scholar Debbie Reese's *American Indians in Children's Literature*, the dozens of articles published in journals like the *Journal for American Indian Education* and the work of the Turtle Island Social Studies Collective, see, as one powerful, award-winning example, Sabzalian, *Indigenous Children's Survivance in Public Schools*.
12. Anna Lees, "Roles of Urban Indigenous Community Members in Collaborative Field-Based Teacher Preparation," *Journal of Teacher Education* 67, no. 5 (November 2016): 363–78; Leilani Sabzalian, "Curricular Standpoints and Native Feminist Theories," 359–82; Meixi et al., "When Learning Is Life Giving."
13. See, among others, Meixi et al., "When Learning Is Life Giving"; Learning in Places (website), accessed May 6, 2022, http://learninginplaces.org/; National Indian Education Association, *Building Relationships with Tribes: A Native Process for ESSA Consultation* (Washington, DC: National Indian Education Association, 2016), http://www.niea.org/for-advocates/education-priorities/state/essa-implementation/niea-consultation-guides/; Christopher Suzanne, Villegas Malia, and Daulton Christina, "'Walk Softly and Listen Carefully': Building Research Relationships with Tribal Communities" (policy paper, Washington, D.C. & Bozeman, MT: NCAI Policy Research Center and MSU Center for Native Health Partnerships, 2012); IllumiNative, *Changing the Narrative About Native*

Americans: A Guide for Allies (n.p.: First Nations Development Institute and Echo Hawk Consulting, 2022), https://illuminative.org/wp-content/uploads/2022/06/MessageGuide-Allies-screen-spreads.pdf.

14. "Americans," Smithsonian National Museum of the American Indian, https://americanindian.si.edu/americans/, accessed October 12, 2024.
15. Stephanie A. Fryberg, et al., "Of Warrior Chiefs and Indian Princesses: The Psychological Consequences of American Indian Mascots," *Basic and Applied Social Psychology* 30, no. 3 (September 26, 2008): 208–18.
16. Anton Treuer, *Everything You Wanted to Know About Indians But Were Afraid to Ask* (n.p.: Borealis Books, 2012).
17. For more on this, see Linda Tuhiwai Smith, *Decolonizing Methodologies: Research and Indigenous Peoples*, 3rd ed. (New York: Bloomsbury Academic, 2022). Other useful overviews of this history and its implications for Western knowledge formation can be found in Audra Simpson, *Mohawk Interruptus: Political Life across the Borders of Settler States* (Durham, NC: Duke University Press, 2014); Cutcha Risling Baldy, *We Are Dancing for You: Native Feminisms and the Revitalization of Women's Coming-of-Age Ceremonies*, 1st ed., Indigenous Confluences (Seattle: University of Washington Press, 2018).
18. Lee Francis IV, writer/host. *Indigi-Genius*. Episode 9, "Cartography." May 24, 2022, PBS. https://www.pbs.org/video/cartography-dks6g0/.
19. "Mapping Indigenous LA," UCLA, https://mila.ss.ucla.edu/; "Projects: Indigenous Chicago," D'Arcy McNickle Center For American Indian And Indigenous Studies, The Newberry, https://www.newberry.org/research/research-centers/mcnickle-center/projects; "Bdote Memory Map," https://bdotememorymap.org/, accessed October 12, 2024
20. Marlena Myles, "Twin Cities Dakota Landmap," https://marlenamyl.es/project/dakota-land-map/.
21. Marlena Myles and Todd Boss, "Dakota Spirit Walk: Augmented Reality Public Art," https://marlenamyl.es/dakota-spirit-walk/.
22. Learning in Places.
23. Shear, Sabzalian, and Snyder, "Rhetorics of Recognition and Erasure."
24. "Northern Plains Treaties," Native Knowledge 360, Smithsonian National Museum of the American Indian, https://americanindian.si.edu/nk360/plains-treaties.
25. Jessica Engelking, *Peggy Flanagan: Ogimaa Kwe, Lieutenant Governor* (Minnesota Humanities Center: Minnesota Native American Lives Series, 2021); Sharice Davids and Nancy K. Mays, *Sharice's Big Voice: A Native Kid Becomes a Congresswoman* (New York: HarperCollins, 2021).
26. Indigenous Journalists Association, https://indigenousjournalists.org/.
27. Matika Wilbur, "About Project 562," https://www.project562.com/about.
28. Nēpia Mahuika, *Rethinking Oral History and Tradition: An Indigenous Perspective*, Oxford Oral History Series (New York, NY: Oxford University Press, 2019).
29. *United Nations Declaration on the Rights of Indigenous Peoples* (New York, NY: United Nations, 2007), https://www.un.org/development/desa/indigenouspeoples/wp-content/uploads/sites/19/2018/11/UNDRIP_E_web.pdf; *Know Your Rights! United Nations Declaration on the Rights of Indigenous Peoples for Indigenous Adolescents* (New York, NY: United Nations Childrens Fund, with UNICEF Human Rights Unit, 2013), https://un-declaration.narf.org/wp-content/uploads/un-adolescents-guide2013.pdf.
30. "Teachings of Our Elders," North Dakota Native American Essential Understandings Project, https://teachingsofourelders.org/interviews-ndnaeu/; "The Oceti-Sakowin Essential Understandings," The WoLakota Project, https://www.wolakotaproject.org/video-interviews/.

31. American Indians in Children's Literature (website), https://americanindiansinchildrensliterature.blogspot.com/; Odia Wood-Krueger, *A Guide To Reliable Native American-Related Teaching Resources: With Reference To Minnesota K–12 Academic Standards in English Language Arts* (Prior Lake, MN: Shakopee Mdewakanton Sioux Community, 2024).

Chapter 4

1. Carter G. Woodson, *The Mis-Education of the Negro* (New York, Penguin, 2023), 75.
2. Brittany L. Jones, "Feeling Fear as Power and Oppression: An Examination of Black and White Fear in Virginia's U.S. History Standards and Curriculum Framework," *Theory & Research in Social Education* (2022): 431.
3. Tomarra A. Adams, "Establishing Intellectual Space for Black Students in Predominately White Universities Through Black Studies," *Negro Educational Review* (2005): 285.
4. Sam Wineburg and Chauncey Monte-Sano, "Famous Americans. The Changing Pantheon of American Heroes," *Journal of American History* 94 (2008): 1186–1202.
5. Jones, "Feeling Fear," 431.
6. LaGarrett J. King, "The Status of Black History in U.S. Schools and Society," *Social Education* (2017): 14–18.
7. Wintre Foxworth Johnson and Jennifer D. Turner, "To Dream, to Fly, and to Be: Depictions of Black Livingness in Contemporary African American Children's Literature," *Language Arts* 101 (2023): 2.
8. Norline R. Wild, "Picture Books for Social Justice: Creating a Classroom Community Grounded in Identity, Diversity, Justice, and Action," *Early Childhood Education Journal* (2022), https://doi.org/10.1007/s10643-022-01342-1.
9. Ryan Hughes, "'What Is Slavery?': Third-Grade Students' Sensemaking about Enslavement Through Historical Inquiry," *Theory & Research in Social Education* 50, no. 1 (2022): 29–73, https://doi.org/10.1080/00933104.2021.1927921.
10. Dawnavyn M. James, *Beyond February: Teaching Black History Any Day, Every Day, and All Year Long, K–3* (New York: Routledge, 2024).
11. John S. Wills, "'Some People Even Died': Martin Luther King, Jr, the Civil Rights Movement and the Politics of Remembrance in Elementary Classrooms," *International Journal of Qualitative Studies in Education* 18, no. 1 (2005), https://doi.org/10.1080/09518390412331318397.
12. *New York State K–8 Social Studies Framework* (Albany: The University of the State of New York, 2017): 16–17.
13. LaGarrett J. King, "Black History is not American History: Toward a Framework of Black Historical Consciousness," *Social Education* 86, no. 6 (2020): 335–41; Brianne Pitts and Dawnavyn James, "Committed to Teaching Black History," *Social Studies and the Young Learner* 35, no. 3 (2023): 13–19.
14. Eduardo Bonilla-Silva, "Feeling Race: Theorizing the Racial Economy of Emotions," *American Sociological Review* 84 (2019): 1–25.
15. Tiffany L. Green and Tod G. Hamilton, "Beyond Black and White: Color and Mortality in Post-Reconstruction Era North Carolina," *Explorations in Economic History* 50, no. 1 (2013): 148–59.
16. Brittany L. Jones, "Learning from Black Perspectives: A Case for Making Space to Feel Race in High School US History Classrooms" (PhD diss., Michigan State University, 2023).
17. Myisha Cherry, *The Case for Rage: Why Anger is Essential to Anti-Racist Struggle* (New York: Oxford University Press, 2021).

18. James Baldwin, "The Negro in American Culture," *Cross Currents,* 11, no. 3 (1961): 205–225, https://www.jstor.org/stable/i24446675.
19. Cornell West, *Race Matters* (Boston: Beacon Press, 2001).
20. Bryan J. McCann, "Affect, Black Rage, and False Alternatives in the Hip-Hop Nation," *Cultural Studies Critical Methodologies* 13, no. 5 (2013): 408–18.
21. William H. Grier and Price M. Cobbs, *Black Rage* (Eugene, OR: Wipf and Stock, 2000).
22. Jones, "Learning from Black Perspectives."
23. Jones, "Learning from Black Perspectives."
24. "Why BH365," Black History 365, 2022, https://blackhistory365education.com/why-bh365/.
25. "Why BH365."
26. Derrick P. Alridge, "The Limits of Master Narratives in History Textbooks: An Analysis of Representations of Martin Luther King, Jr.," *Teachers College Record* (2006): 662–86.
27. John B. Nezlek and Peter Kuppens, "Regulating Positive and Negative Emotions in Daily Life," *Journal of Personality,* 76 no. 3 (2008): 561–80.
28. Walter Milton and Joel A. Freeman, *Black History 365: African Americans Shaping a Nation*, (Arlington, TX: CGW365 Publishing, 2021), 35.
29. Milton and Freeman, *Black History 365*, 44, 48, 50, 51.
30. Milton and Freeman, *Black History 365*, 12, 14.
31. Milton and Freeman, *Black History 365*, 14.
32. Milton and Freeman, *Black History 365*, 58, 59.
33. Milton and Freeman, *Black History 365*, 59.
34. Baldwin, "The Negro in American Culture," 205.
35. Milton and Freeman, *Black History 365*, 35.
36. Milton and Freeman, *Black History 365*, 35.
37. John Lovell, "The Social Implications of the Negro Spiritual," *Journal of Negro Education*, 8 no. 4 (1939): 634–43.
38. Jones, "Feeling Fear."
39. Robert J. Jagers, Deborah Rivas-Drake, and Brittney Williams, "Transformative Social and Emotional Learning (SEL): Toward SEL in Service of Educational Equity and Excellence," *Educational Psychologist* 54, no. 3 (2019): 162–84, https://doi.org/10.1080/00461520.2019.1623032; Jones, "Learning from Black Perspectives."
40. Milton and Freeman, *Black History 365*, 67.
41. James Brown, vocalist, "Say It Loud—I'm Black and I'm Proud," by James Brown and Alfred Ellis, Universal Studios, 1969, vinyl.
42. Maribel Santiago and Tadashi Dozono, "History is Critical: Addressing the False Dichotomy Between Historical Inquiry and Criticality," *Theory & Research in Social Education* (2022): 183.
43. Tadashi Dozono, "Race and the Evidence of Experience: Accounting for Race in Historical Thinking Pedagogy," *Critical Studies in Education* (2022): 468.
44. Dozono, "Race and the Evidence of Experience," 468.
45. Jason Endacott and Sarah Brooks, "An Updated Theoretical and Practical Model for Promoting Historical Empathy," *Social Studies Research and Practice* (2013): 41.

Chapter 5

1. There are many terms that one can use to describe "people of color." It is our opinion that none of them achieves the elusive goal of remaining inclusive of the many communities they

are intended to encompass while also acknowledging their distinct and complex identities and experiences. When referring to minoritized racial and ethnic peoples in the United States, we name them specifically rather than elide some of them under the potentially essentializing banner of "people of color." We respect others' decisions to opt for other labels.

2. Robin Bernstein, *Racial Innocence* (New York: New York University Press, 2011); T. Elon Dancy II, "(Un)Doing Hegemony in Education: Disrupting School-to-Prison Pipelines for Black Males," *Equity & Excellence in Education* 47, no. 4 (2014): 476–93; Phillip A. Goff, Jennifer L. Eberhardt, Melissa J. Williams, and Matthew C. Jackson, "Not Yet Human: Implicit Knowledge, Historical Dehumanization, and Contemporary Consequences," *Journal of Personality and Social Psychology* 94, no. 2 (2008): 292; Phillip A. Goff, Matthew C. Jackson, Brooke A. Lewis Di Leone, Carmen M. Culotta, and Natalie A. DiTomasso, "The Essence of Innocence: Consequences of Dehumanizing Black Children," *Journal of Personality and Social Psychology* 106, no. 4 (2014): 526.
3. We use the terms AfroLatinx and AfroIndigenous interchangeably throughout this chapter while also recognizing that these terms sometimes carry different histories and interpretations. "Afro" is an important point of connection and a way of naming shared struggles and cultures, particularly as they find historical and cultural grounding on the African continent: Miriam Jiménez Román and Juan Flores, eds., *The Afro-Latin@ Reader: History and Culture in the United States* (Durham, NC: Duke University Press, 2010).
4. Sharlene Mollett, "Race and Natural Resource Conflicts in Honduras: The Miskito and Garifuna Struggle for Lasa Pulan," *Latin American Research Review* 41, no. 1 (2006): 96.
5. Agustin Lao Montes, "Decolonial Moves: Trans-locating African Diaspora Spaces," *Cultural Studies* 21, no. 23 (March/May 2007): 318.
6. We are skeptical of the moniker "America" because of its European origins and common construction of the United States as constituting "America." Nonetheless, we use "United States" and other national place names to denote the territories that the Declaración de Kito agrees to call "Abya Yala," meaning "mature land" in the language of the Guna people that inhabit Panama and Colombia.
7. We do not italicize words in the Spanish language because Spanish is no more a "foreign" language in these lands than English is. In fact, Spanish predates English in the United States since it was spoken here as early as the founding of the first permanent colony at San Agustín, Florida, in 1565. Both are colonial languages.
8. Milagros Ricourt, *The Dominican Racial Imaginary: Surveying the Landscape of Race and Nation in Hispaniola* (New Brunswick, NJ: Rutgers University Press, 2016).
9. Andrew Lawler, "Church Unearthed in Ethiopia Rewrites the History of Christianity in Africa," *Smithsonian Magazine*, December 2019; Jennifer Williams, "From Aset to Jesus: The History of the Goddess Aset in Ancient Kemet from Circa 3000 BCE Until the Removal of Feminine Salvation Circa 400 CE," *Journal of Black Studies* 45, no. 2 (2014): 102–24.
10. Krista L. Cortes, "'Brujería Lite': Centering Blackness-as-Practice in Everyday AfroPuerto Rican Spiritualities," *Centro Journal* 33, no. 3 (2021): 128–57.
11. Marta Morena Vega, "The Ancestral Sacred Creative Impulse of Africa and the African Diaspora: Ase, The Nexus of the Black Global Aesthetic," *Lenox Avenue: A Journal of Interarts Inquiry* 5 (1999): 340, https://doi.org/10.2307/4177077.
12. Juan Flores and Miriam Jiménez Román, "Triple-Consciousness? Approaches to Afro-Latino Culture in the United States," *Latin American and Caribbean Ethnic Studies* 4, no. 3 (2009):

319–328; David Sikkink and Edwin Hernández, *Religion Matters: Predicting Schooling Success Among Latino Youth* (South Bend, IN: Institute for Latino Studies, January 2003).

13. Helen Rose Ebaugh and Mary Curry, "Fictive Kin as Social Capital in New Immigrant Communities," *Sociological Perspectives* 43 (2000): 189–209, https://doi.org/10.2307/1389793.
14. Theresa Delgadillo, "Spirituality," in *The Routledge Companion to Latino/a Literature*, ed. Suzanne Bost and Frances Aparicio (New York: Routledge, 2012), 240–250; Antonio M. Stevens-Arroyo and Andrés Isidro Perez y Mena, *Enigmatic Powers: Syncretism with African and Indigenous Peoples' Religions Among Latinos* (New York, NY: Bildner Center for the Western Hemisphere Studies, 1995).
15. Cortes, "'Brujería Lite.'"
16. Krista L. Cortes, "AfroBoriqua Mothering: Teaching/Learning Blackness in a Bay Area AfroPuerto Rican Community of Practice," *Journal of Cultural and Ethnic Studies* 7, no. 2 (2020): 127–146, https://doi.org/10.29333/ejecs/351; George J. Sefa Dei, *Teaching Africa: Towards a Transgressive Pedagogy* (New York: Springer, 2010).
17. Carlyle Fielding Stewart, *Black Spirituality and Black Consciousness: Soul Force, Culture and Freedom in the African American Experience* (Trenton, NJ: Africa World Press, 1999); Miguel A. De La Torre, *Santeria: The Beliefs and Rituals of a Growing Religion in America* (Grand Rapids, MI: William B. Eerdmans, 2004); Marta Moreno Vega, Alba Marinieves and Yvette Modestin, *Women Warriors of the Afro-Latina Diaspora* (Houston, TX: Arte Público Press, 2012).
18. De La Torre, *Santeria*.
19. Dorothy Holland et al., *Agency and Identity in Cultural Worlds* (Cambridge, MA: Harvard University Press, 1998); Na'ilah Suad Nasir, "When Development Is Not Universal: Understanding the Unique Developmental Tasks that Race, Gender, and Social Class Impose: Commentary on Rogers and Way," *Human Development* 61, no. 6 (2019): 332–36.
20. Shirin Vossoughi and Kris D. Gutiérrez, "Studying Movement, Hybridity, and Change: Toward a Multi-Sited Sensibility for Research on Learning Across Contexts and Borders," *Teachers College Record* 116, no. 14 (2014): 603–32; Vossoughi and Gutiérrez, "Studying Movement."
21. Vossoughi and Gutiérrez, "Studying Movement."
22. Kris D. Gutiérrez, "Integrative Research Review: Syncretic Approaches to Literacy Learning. Leveraging Horizontal Knowledge and Expertise," *63rd Literacy Research Association Yearbook* (2014): 49.
23. Kris D. Gutiérrez and A. Susan Jurow, "Social Design Experiments: Toward Equity by Design," *Journal of the Learning Sciences* 25, no. 4 (2016): 573, https://doi.org/10.1080/10508406.2016.1204548.
24. Gutiérrez and Jurow, "Social Design Experiments," 567.
25. Gutiérrez and Jurow, "Social Design Experiments," 567.
26. Kris D. Gutiérrez, "Designing Resilient Ecologies: Social Design Experiments and a New Social Imagination," *Educational Researcher* 45, no. 3 (2016): 187–96; Kris D. Gutiérrez et al., "Youth as Historical Actors in the Production of Possible Futures," *Mind, Culture, and Activity* 26, no. 4 (2019): 291–308; Django Paris and H. Samy Alim, eds., *Culturally Sustaining Pedagogies: Teaching and Learning for Justice in a Changing World* (New York, NY: Teachers College Press, 2017).
27. Zamokwakho Hlela, "Learning Through the Action of Research: Reflections on an Afrocentric Research Design," *Community Development Journal* 53, no. 2 (2018): 375–92.

28. Yomaira C. Figueroa-Vásquez, *Decolonizing Diasporas: Radical Mappings of Afro-Atlantic Literature* (Chicago, IL: Northwestern University Press, 2020).
29. Lao Montes, "Decolonial Moves."
30. Yomaira C. Figueroa, "Your Lips: Mapping Afro-Boricua Feminist Becomings," *Frontiers: A Journal of Women Studies* 41, no. 1 (2020): 2.
31. bell hooks, *Teaching to Transgress* (New York, NY: Routledge, 1994).

Chapter 6

1. Edward W. Said, *Orientalism* (New York, NY: Vintage Books, 1979), pxviii.
2. The Nakba (Al-Nakba, "The Catastrophe") is the Arabic term used to refer to the massacres, displacement, dispossession, and expulsion of Palestinians during the colonial creation of the Zionist Israeli state in 1948. Between 1947 and 1949, more than 750,000 Palestinians were ethnically cleansed from over 530 villages, towns, and cities in Palestine. To learn more about the Nakba, see Rashid Khalidi, *The Hundred Years' War on Palestine: A History of Settler Colonialism and Resistance, 1917–2017* (New York: Metropolitan Books, 2020); Ilan Pappé, *The Ethnic Cleansing of Palestine* (Oxford: Oneworld, 2007); Ahmad H. Sa'di and Lila Abu-Lughod, *Nakba: Palestine, 1948, and the Claims of Memory* (New York, NY: Columbia University Press, 2007); and Rosemary Sayigh, "Self-Recording of a National Disaster: Oral History and the Palestinian Nakba," *Journal of Holy Land and Palestinian Studies* 19, no. 1 (2020): 1–13.
3. Mughar Al-Khayt is the placename of my family's now depopulated village in the Safad district in Northern Palestine. Palestinians often assert that the Nakba never ended; it continues through ongoing colonization, ethnic cleansing, apartheid, and militarized violence and oppression.
4. Edward Said, "The Idea of Palestine in the West," *MERIP Reports*, no. 70 (1978).
5. Isabelle Humphries and Laleh Khalili, "Gender of Nakba Memory," in *Nakba: Palestine, 1948, and the Claims of Memory*, ed. Ahmad H. Sa'di and Lila Abu-Lughod (New York: Columbia University Press, 2007); Fatma Kassem, *Palestinian Women: Narrative Histories and Gendered Memory* (London: Zed Books, 2011); and Nadera Shalhoub-Kevorkian, "Palestinian Women and the Politics of Invisibility: Towards a Feminist Methodology," *Peace Prints: South Asian Journal of Peacebuilding* 3, no. 1 (2010): 1–21.
6. Ahmad H. Sa'di, "Afterword: Reflections on Representations, History, and Moral Accountability," in *Nakba: Palestine, 1948, and the Claims of Memory*, ed. Ahmad H. Sa'di and Lila Abu-Lughod (New York: Columbia University Press, 2007), 285–314.
7. Sa'di, "Afterword," 286.
8. Edward Said, "Permission to Narrate," *Journal of Palestine Studies* 13, no. 3 (1984): 27–48.
9. Said, "Permission to Narrate," 27.
10. Said, "The Idea of Palestine," 11.
11. Nur Masalha, *The Palestine Nakba: Decolonising History, Narrating the Subaltern, Reclaiming Memory* (New York: Bloomsbury, 2012), 218.
12. Linda Tuhiwai Smith, *Decolonizing Methodologies: Research and Indigenous Peoples*, 3rd ed. (London: Zed Books, 2021).
13. Smith, *Decolonizing Methodologies*, 38.
14. Rosemary Sayigh, "Nakba Silencing and the Challenge of Palestinian Oral History," in *An Oral History of the Palestinian Nakba*, ed. Nahla Abdo and Nur Masalha (New York: Bloomsbury, 2018).

15. Yasmeen Abu-Laban and Abigail B. Bakan, "Anti-Palestinian Racism: Analyzing the Unnamed and Suppressed Reality," *Project on Middle East Political Science (POMEPS)* 44, no. 1 (2021): 143–49; Yasmeen Abu-Laban and Abigail B. Bakan, "Anti-Palestinian Racism and Racial Gaslighting," *Political Quarterly* 93, no. 3 (2022): 508–16; Dania Majid, *Anti-Palestinian Racism: Naming, Framing and Manifestations* (n.p.: Arab Canadian Lawyers Association, 2022); Sa'di and Abu-Lughod, *Nakba: Palestine*; Peige Desjarlais, "The Violence of Representation: The (Un) Narration of Palestine in Public Discursive Space in Canada" (master's thesis, University of Western Ontario, 2014).
16. Sayigh, "Self-Recording: Oral History," 5.
17. See, for example, David Stovall, "Are We Ready for 'School' Abolition?: Thoughts and Practices of Radical Imaginary in Education," *Taboo: The Journal of Culture and Education* 17, no.1 (2018): 51–61.
18. See Abu-Laban and Bakan, "Anti-Palestinian Racism: Analyzing the Unnamed"; Abu-Laban and Bakan, "Anti-Palestinian Racism and Racial Gaslighting"; and Majid, *Anti-Palestinian Racism: Naming.*
19. Majid, *Anti-Palestinian Racism: Naming*, 14.
20. It is important to note that not all Muslims are Arab (fewer than 20 percent of Muslims worldwide are Arab), and not all Arabs are Muslim (although over 90 percent identify as Muslim).
21. Yasmeen Abu-Laban, "On the Borderlines of Human and Citizen: The Liminal State of Arab Canadians," in *Targeted Transnationals: The State, the Media, and Arab Canadians*, ed. Jenna Hennebry and Bessma Momani (Vancouver, BC: UBC Press, 2013), 68–85; Steven Salaita, *Anti-Arab Racism in the USA: Where it Comes from and What it Means Today* (London: Pluto Press, 2006); Abu-Laban and Bakan, "Anti-Palestinian Racism: Analyzing the Unnamed."
22. See Thea Randa Abu El-Haj, *Unsettled Belonging: Educating Palestinian American Youth After 9/11* (Chicago: University of Chicago Press, 2015); Cole, "Under Investigation: Anti-Palestinian Racism"; Muslim Engagement and Development (MEND), "Schools punishing students for supporting Palestine, including exclusions and calling police," June 25, 2021, https://www.mend.org.uk/mend-press-release-schools-punishing-students-for-supporting-palestine-including-exclusions-and-calling-police/; and Palestine Legal, *The Palestine Exception to Free Speech: A Movement Under Attack in the US* (n.p.: Center for Constitutional Rights, 2015).
23. Desmond Cole, "Under Investigation: Anti-Palestinian Racism at the Toronto District School Board," *Yes Everything*, October 7, 2021, para. 1.
24. Bruce Frisco and Alex MacIsaac, "Protesters Call for Investigation after Palestinian Students Told to Take Off Traditional Scarves at Halifax School," *CTV News Atlantic*, March 6, 2023, para. 3; Frisco and MacIsaac, "Protesters Call for Investigation," para. 9.
25. Hanadi Shatara, "Critical Political Consciousness within Nepantla as Transformative: The Experiences and Pedagogy of a Palestinian World History Teacher," *Curriculum Inquiry* 53, no. 1 (2022a): 28–48.
26. Pseudonyms used for youth participants. Also, see "What's Behind the Ramadan Raids at Jerusalem's Al-Aqsa Mosque?" *Aljazeera*, April 5, 2023, https://aje.io/b6wef0.
27. Kassem, *Palestinian Women: Narrative Histories*, 10.
28. Smith, *Decolonizing Methodologies*, xii.
29. Smith, *Decolonizing Methodologies*, xii.
30. Smith, *Decolonizing Methodologies*, 33.

31. Smith, *Decolonizing Methodologies*, 32.
32. Lena Jayyusi, "The Time of Small Returns: Affect and Resistance During the Nakba" in *An Oral History of the Palestinian Nakba*, ed. Nahla Abdo and Nur Masalha (New York: Bloomsbury, 2018), 107.
33. Nur Masalha, "Remembering the Palestinian Nakba: Commemoration, Oral History and Narratives of Memory," *Holy Land Studies* 7, no. 2 (2008): 138.
34. Sayigh, "Nakba Silencing," 123.
35. Farah Aboubakr Alkhammash, "The Folktale as a Site of Framing Palestinian Memory and Identity in Speak, Bird, Speak Again and Qul Ya Tayer" (PhD diss., University of Manchester, 2014), 22; Yara Hawari, "Palestine Sine Tempore?" *Rethinking History* 22, no. 2 (2018), 165–83; Masalha, *Palestine Nakba*; Sayigh, "Nakba Silencing"; Sayigh, "Self-Recording: Oral History."
36. Masalha, "Decolonizing Methodology, Reclaiming Memory," 27.
37. Hawari, "Palestine Sine Tempore."
38. Madeeha Hafez Albatta, *A White Lie: Women's Voices from Gaza*, ed. Barbara Bill and Ghada Ageel (Edmonton, AB: University of Alberta Press, 2020), XLIII.
39. Kassem, *Palestinian Women: Narrative Histories*, 195.
40. Kassem, *Palestinian Women: Narrative Histories*, 195.
41. Rosemary Sayigh, "Women's Nakba Stories: Between Being and Knowing," in *Nakba: Palestine, 1948, and the Claims of Memory*, ed. Ahmad H. Sa'di and Lila Abu-Lughod (New York: Columbia University Press, 2007), 138.
42. Noura Erakat, *Justice for Some: Law and the Question of Palestine* (Stanford: Stanford University Press, 2019).
43. Kassem, *Palestinian Women: Narrative Histories*; and Rosemary Sayigh, "Afterword: Oral History in Palestinian Studies," in *Voices of the Nakba: A Living History of Palestine*, ed. Diana Allan (London: Pluto Press, 2021), 293–300.
44. Rosemary Sayigh, "Where Are the History Books for Palestinian Children?" *Journal of Holy Land and Palestine Studies* 16, no. 2 (2017): 145.
45. Sayigh, "Where are the History Books," 145–46.
46. Echoing Palestinians, on October 13, 2023, Israeli Historian and Holocaust and genocide scholar Raz Segal named the Israeli regime's horrific war against the people of Gaza as "a textbook case of genocide." Raz Segal, "A Textbook Case of Genocide: Israel Has Been Explicit About What It's Carrying Out in Gaza. Why Isn't The World Listening?" *Jewish Currents*, October 13, 2023, https://jewishcurrents.org/a-textbook-case-of-genocide. This was months before the genocide of at least 35,562 Palestinians in Gaza as of May 20, 2024 (United Nations Office for the Coordination of Humanitarian Affairs [OCHA]), "Hostilities in the Gaza Strip and Israel Flash Update #168," OCHA in the occupied Palestinian territory (oPt), May 20, 2024, https://www.ochaopt.org/content/hostilities-gaza-strip-and-israel-flash-update-168). This was also months before South Africa's December 29, 2023, application of the Convention on the Prevention and Punishment of the Crime of Genocide in the Gaza Strip against Israel in the International Court of Justice (ICJ). See International Court of Justice, "The Republic of South Africa Institutes Proceedings Against the State of Israel and Requests the Court to Indicate Provisional Measures," Press Release, December 29, 2023, https://www.icj-cij.org/sites/default/files/case-related/192/192-20231229-pre-01-00-en.pdf. Sophicide is "the annihilation of intellectual and cultural sources of wisdom." Palestinian Feminist Collective, "A Feminist Praxis for Academic Freedom in the Context of Genocide in Gaza," *Mondoweiss*, April 12, 2023, para. 1. Originally conceptualized by

Palestinian scholar Karma Nabulsi, scholasticide refers to "the physical destruction of centers of knowledge, educational resources, infrastructures, and archives as well as the silencing, censorship, and repression of Palestinian history, epistemology, scholarship, and subjectivity" (Palestinian Feminist Collective, "A Feminist Praxis," para. 3).

47. "Palestinian Oral History Archive," American University of Beirut, last accessed October 9, 2024, https://libraries.aub.edu.lb/poha/.
48. "Palestinian Oral History Map," American University of Beirut, last accessed October 9, 2024, https://libraries.aub.edu.lb/poha-viewer/map/en/.
49. Nabka Archive, last accessed October 9, 2024, https://www.nakba-archive.org/.
50. Nancy Kalow and Duke University Center for Documentary Studies, "Palestinian Oral History Project, 2017–2020," last updated March 2022, https://archives.lib.duke.edu/catalog/palestinianoralhistoryproject.
51. Project 48, last accessed October 9, 2024, https://project48.com/.
52. "Teach Palestine," Middle East Children's Alliance, last accessed October 9, 2024, https://teachpalestine.org/resources/videos/.
53. See Gregory Cajete, *Native Science: Natural Laws of Interdependence* (Santa Fe, NM: Clear Light, 2000).
54. Shatara, "Existence is Resistance."
55. Masalha, *Palestine Nakba*, 257.

Chapter 7

1. Angela Valenzuela, *Subtractive Schooling: U.S. Mexican Youth and the Politics of Caring* (Albany, NY: State University of New York Press, 1999).
2. Samuel Bowles and Herbert Gintis, *Schooling in Capitalist America: Educational Reform and the Contradictions of Economic Life* (New York, NY: Basic Books, 1976).
3. Leny Mendoza Strobel, *Coming Full Circle: The Process of Decolonization Among Post-1965 Filipino Americans*, 2nd ed. (United States: CreateSpace Independent Publishing Platform, 2016).
4. Damiana L. Eugenio, *Philippine Folk Literature: An Anthology*, 2nd ed. (Diliman, Quezon City: University of the Philippines Press, 2007).
5. Korina M. Jocson, "Kuwento as Multicultural Pedagogy in High School Ethnic Studies," *Pedagogies: An International Journal* 3, no. 4 (2008): 241–53.
6. Tara Yosso, "Whose Culture Has Capital? A Critical Race Theory Discussion of Community Cultural Wealth," *Race Ethnicity and Education* 8, no. 1 (2005): 69–91.
7. Roderick Daus-Magbual, "Brown Washing Hermeneutics: Historically Responsive Pedagogy in Ethnic Studies," in *"White" Washing American Education: The New Culture Wars in Ethnic Studies*, ed. Denise M. Sandoval, Anthony J. Ratcliff, Tracy Lachica Buenavista, and James R. Marín (Santa Barbara: Praeger, 2016), 199–221.
8. Teresa L. McCarty and Sheilah E. Nicholas, "Reclaiming Indigenous Languages: A Reconsideration of the Roles and Responsibilities of Schools," *Review of Research in Education* 38 (2014): 106–36.
9. Valerie Francisco, "'Ang Ating Iisang Kuwento' Our Collective Story: Migrant Filipino Workers and Participatory Action Research," *Action Research* 12, no. 1 (2014): 78–93.
10. Rose Ann Gutierrez, Hazel Piñon, and Marie Trisha Valmocena, "Co-Creating Knowledge with Undocumented Filipino Students: *Kuwentuhan* as a Research Method," *New Directions for Higher Education* 2023, no. 203 (2023): 84–88.
11. Paulo Freire, *Pedagogy of the Oppressed* (New York: Seabury Press, 1970).

12. Francisco, "'Ang Ating Iisang Kuwento,'" 80; Valerie Francisco-Menchavez, "Kuwentuhan as a Method: Migrant Filipino Workers and Participatory Action Research," *Handbook of Social Inclusion* (2022), 1527; Gutierrez, Piñon, and Valmocena, "Co-Creating Knowledge," 84.
13. Jeannie Estella Celestial, "Trauma," in *The SAGE Encyclopedia of Filipina/x/o American Studies*, ed. Kevin Leo Yabut Nadal, Allyson Tintiangco-Cubales, and E.J.R. David (Thousand Oaks, CA: SAGE Publications, 2022), 2: 975–80.
14. Celestial, "Trauma," 977.
15. Lauren Arzaga Daus, "Immigration and Nationality Act of 1965," in *The SAGE Encyclopedia of Filipina/x/o American Studies*, ed. Kevin Leo Yabut Nadal, Allyson Tintiangco-Cubales, and E.J.R. David (Thousand Oaks, CA: SAGE Publications, Inc., 2022), 2: 534–36.
16. Alyssa Hufana, "Historical Trauma," in *The SAGE Encyclopedia of Filipina/x/o American Studies*, eds. Kevin Leo Yabut Nadal, Allyson Tintiangco-Cubales, and E.J.R. David (Thousand Oaks, CA: SAGE Publications, Inc., 2022), 1:496.
17. Gutierrez, Piñon, and Valmocena, "Co-Creating Knowledge," 86.
18. D. Jean Clandinin and F. Michael Connelly, *Narrative Inquiry: Experience and Story in Qualitative Research* (Hoboken, NJ: Jossey-Bass, 2000); Ananda Marin, Katie Headrick Taylor, Ben Rydal Shapiro, and Rogers Hall, "Why Learning on the Move: Intersecting Research Pathways for Mobility, Learning and Teaching," *Cognition and Instruction* 38, no. 3 (2020): 265–80; Ann Phoenix and Marjorie Faulstich Orellana, "Adult Narratives of Childhood Language Brokering: Learning What It Means to Be Bilingual," *Children & Society* 36, no. 3 (2021): 386–99.
19. Lauren Arzaga Daus, "United in Grief: Teachers of Color Engaging in Love, Humanization, and Radical Joy," *Journal of Trauma Studies in Education* 2, no. 3 (2023): 102–117.
20. Daus, "United in Grief," 106.
21. Gutierrez, Piñon, and Valmocena, "Co-Creating Knowledge," 87.
22. Rebecca Walker, "Becoming the 3rd Wave," *ProQuest Central* 12, no. 2 (2002): 86–87.
23. Kris D. Gutiérrez, Patricia Baquedano-López, and Carlos Tejada, "Rethinking Diversity: Hybridity and Hybrid Language Practices in the Third Space," *Mind, Culture, and Activity* 6, no. 4 (1999): 286–303.
24. Amado M. Padilla, "Ethnic Minority Scholars, Research, and Mentoring: Current and Future Issues," *Educational Researcher* 23, no. 4 (1994): 24–27.
25. William A. Smith, "Higher Education: Racial Battle Fatigue," *Encyclopedia of Race, Ethnicity, and Society* (2008): 615–618.
26. Gutierrez, Piñon, and Valmocena, "Co-Creating Knowledge," 77–92.
27. Jocson, "Kuwento as Multicultural Pedagogy," 243.
28. Jocson, "Kuwento as Multicultural Pedagogy," 245.
29. Jocson, "Kuwento as Multicultural Pedagogy," 246.
30. Jocson, "Kuwento as Multicultural Pedagogy," 250.
31. *History-Social Science Content Standards* (Sacremento: California Department of Education, 2000), https://www.cde.ca.gov/be/st/ss/documents/histsocscistnd.pdf.
32. Allyson Tintiangco-Cubales, "Pinayism," *Maganda Magazine* (1995).
33. Jocson, "Kuwento as Multicultural Pedagogy," 242.
34. Jocson, "Kuwento as Multicultural Pedagogy," 243.
35. Allyson Tintiangco-Cubales and Jocyl Sacramento, "Pin[a/x]yism Revisited: A Pedagogical Praxis toward Collective Liberation," in *Closer to Liberation: Pin[a/x]y Activism in Theory and Practice*, ed. Amanda Solomon Amorao, DJ Kuttin Kandi, and Jen Soriano (San Diego, CA: Cognella, 2023), xlviii–lx.

36. This is a sample schedule for a project and not a complete syllabus or curriculum. This schedule is meant to be illustrative.
37. Ramón Grosfoguel, "The Structure of Knowledge in Westernized Universities: Epistemic Racism/Sexism and the Four Genocides/Epistemicides of the Long 16th Century," *Human Architecture: Journal of the Sociology of Self-Knowledge* 11, no. 1 (2013): 73–90.
38. Dolores Delgado Bernal, Rebeca Burciaga, and Judith Flores Carmona, "Chicana/Latina Testimonios: Mapping the Methodological, Pedagogical, and Political," *Equity & Excellence in Èducation* 45, no. 3 (2012): 363–372; Sharim Hannegan-Martinez, "Pláticas as a Methodological Praxis of Love," *International Journal of Qualitative Studies in Education* 36, no. 9 (2023): 1702–13.
39. Shawn Wilson, *Research is Ceremony: Indigenous Research Method* (Halifax: Fernwood Publishing, 2008); Jo-ann Archibald, *Indigenous Storywork: Educating The Heart, Mind, Body, And Spirit* (Vancouver: UBC Press, 2014); Linda Tuhiwai Smith, *Decolonizing Methodologies: Research and Indigenous Peoples*, 2nd ed. (London: Zed Books, 2012).
40. Francisco-Menchavez, "Kuwentuhan as a Method," 1528.
41. Virgilio G. Enriquez, *From Colonial to Liberation Psychology: The Philippine Experience* (Manila: De La Salle University Press, 2004).

Chapter 8

1. Maya Chinchilla, *The Cha Cha Files: A Chapina Poética* (San Francisco: Kórima Press, 2014).
2. Maya Chinchilla, "Maya Like the People," in *The Cha Cha Files: A Chapina Poética* (San Francisco: Kórima Press, 2014), 27.
3. To read more historical examples of Central American Testimonio, see Gioconda Belli, *The Country Under My Skin* (London: Bloomsbury Paperbacks, 2003); Óscar A Romero, *The Violence of Love*, trans. James R Brockman (Maryknoll, NY: Orbis Books, 2004); Roque Dalton, *Revolución en la revolución?: y la crítica de derecha* (Havana, Cuba: Casa de las Américas, 1970); Roberto Lovato, *Unforgetting: A Memoir of Family, Migration, Gangs, and Revolution in the Americas* (New York: Harper, 2020); Óscar Martínez Peñate, *El Salvador, El Soldado y la Guerrillera: Historia y Relatos de Vida* (self-pub., 2008); Victor Montejo, *Testimony: Death of a Guatemalan Village* (New York: Curbstone Press, 1995); Rigoberta Menchu, *Rigoberta Menchu: An Indian Woman in Guatemala* (New York: Verso, 1994).
4. See Rigoberta Menchu, *Rigoberta Menchu*; Linda Tuhiwai Smith, *Decolonizing Methodologies: Research and Indigenous Peoples* (London: Zed Books, 2012).
5. Dolores Delgado Bernal, Rebeca Burciaga, and Judith Flores Carmona, "Chicana/Latina *Testimonios*: Mapping Methodological, Pedagogical, and Political Urgency," *Equity & Excellence in Education* 45, no. 3 (2012): 363–72, https://www.tandfonline.com/doi/abs/10.1080/10665684.2012.698149.
6. Lindsay Pérez Huber and Bert María Cueva, "Chicana/Latina *Testimonios* on Effects and Responses to Microaggressions," *Equity & Excellence in Education* 45, no. 3 (2012): 392–410, https://doi.org/10.1080/10665684.2012.698193.
7. Paulo Freire, *Pedagogy of the Oppressed* (New York: Bloomsbury Academic, 1970).
8. Cherríe Moraga and Gloria Anzaldúa, *This Bridge Called My Back: Writings by Radical Women of Color* (Albany: State University of New York Press, 2005).
9. Shawn Ginwright, *Hope and Healing in Urban Education* (New York: Routledge, 2015).
10. Shawn Ginwright, "The Future of Healing: Shifting from Trauma Informed Care to Healing Centered Engagement," *Medium*, May 31, 2018, https://medium.com/@ginwright

/the-future-of-healingshifting-from-trauma-informed-care-to-healing-centered-engagement-634f557ce69c.

11. Shawn Ginwright, "The Future of Healing."
12. bell hooks, *Yearning: Race, Gender, and Cultural Politics* (New York: Routledge, 1990).
13. Steven Mayers and Jonathan Freedman, *Solito, Solita Crossing Borders with Youth Refugees from Central America* (Chicago, IL: Haymarket Books, 2019).
14. For examples of Central American youth testimonios see Sonia Nazario, *Enrique's Journey: The True Story of a Boy Determined to Reunite with His Mother* (New York: Delacorte Books, 2014); Juan Pablo Villalobos, *The Other Side: Stories of Central American Teen Refugees Who Dream of Crossing the Border*, trans. Rosalind Harvey (New York: Farrar Straus Giroux, 2019); Latino Youth Leadership Council of LAYC, *Voces Sin Fronteras: Our Stories, Our Truth (New Foreword by Meg Medina)* (Washington D.C.: Shout Mouse Press, 2018).
15. Plàticas or the act of platicando refers to informal conversations which, in Latin American communities, typically occur in salas (living rooms), at kitchen tables, and in other gathering spaces. The knowledge of every person participating is acknowledged and shared through dichos (sayings), consejos (advice), chismes, and testimonios. For more information, see Monica Ybarra, "'We Have a Strong Way of Thinking . . . and It Shows through Our Words': Exploring Mujerista Literacies with Chicana/Latina Youth in a Community Ethnic Studies Course," *Research in the Teaching of English* 54, no. 3 (2020): 231–53; Joseph P. Zanoni, "Dialogue and Hegemony: Sociolinguistic Analysis of 'Charlas' for Critique and Praxis," *Mediterranean Journal of Educational Studies* 13, no. 1 (2008): 39–58; Cindy O. Fierros and Dolores Delgado Bernal, "Vamos a Platicar: The Contours Of Pláticas as Chicana/Latina Feminist Methodology," *Chicana/Latina Studies* 15, no. 2 (2016): 98–121.
16. adrienne maree brown, "home, love, vulnerability, life," *adrienne maree brown* (blog), June 15, 2014, http://adriennemareebrown.net/2014/06/15/home-love-vulnerability-life/#:~:text=without%20trying%20to%20control%20or.
17. Belli, *The Country Under My Skin.*
18. Belli, *The Country Under My Skin*, 51.
19. María del Carmen Salazar, "A Humanizing Pedagogy," *Review of Research in Education* 37, no. 1 (2013): 121–148, https://doi.org/10.3102/0091732x12464032.
20. Freire, *Pedagogy of the Oppressed*, 17.
21. Gholnecsar E Muhammad, "Protest, Power, and Possibilities: The Need for Agitation Literacies," *Journal of Adolescent & Adult Literacy* 63, no. 3 (2019): 351–55.
22. National Council for the Social Studies (NCSS), *The College, Career, and Civic Life (C3) Framework for Social Studies State Standards* (Silver Spring, MD: NCSS, 2013).
23. Sam Wineburg, *Historical Thinking and Other Unnatural Acts* (Philadelphia, PA: Temple University Press, 2001).
24. For more research on the teaching of immigration, see Wayne Journell, "Setting Out the (Un) Welcome Mat: A Portrayal of Immigration in State Standards for American History," *Social Studies* 100, no. 4, 160–68; Jeremy Hillburn and Ashley Taylor Jaffee, "Teaching Immigration as a Social Issue in 21st-Century Social Studies Classrooms" in *Teaching Social Studies in an Era of Divisiveness: The Challenges of Discussing Social Issues in a Non-Partisan Way*, ed. Wayne Journell (New York: Rowman and Littlefield, 2016), 47–62. For more research on the teaching of Latinx communities, see Edgar Díaz and Matthew R. Deroo, "Latinxs in Contention: A Systemic Functional Linguistic Analysis of 11th-Grade U.S. History Textbooks," *Theory & Research in Social Education* 48, no. 3 (2020), 375–402; Christopher L. Busey, "Más que Esclavos: A BlackCrit Examination of the Treatment of

Afro-Latin@s in US High School World History Textbooks," *Journal of Latinos and Education* 18, (2017): 197–214; Maribel Santiago and Eliana Castro, "Teaching Anti-Essentialist Historical Inquiry," *Social Studies* 110, no. 4 (2019): 170–79; Christopher L. Busey and William B. Russell III, "'We Want to Learn': Middle School Latino/a Students Discuss Social Studies Curriculum and Pedagogy," *RMLE Online* 39, no. 4 (2016): 1–20; Maribel Santiago, "Erasing Differences for the Sake of Inclusion: How Mexican/Mexican American Students Construct Historical Narratives," *Theory & Research in Social Education* 45, no. 1 (2017): 43–74.

25. For more on U.S. intervention in the region, see Walter LaFeber, *Inevitable Revolutions: The United States in Central America* (New York: W.W. Norton, 1993); María Cristina García, *Seeking Refuge: Central American Migration to Mexico, the United States and Canada* (California: University of California Press, 2006); Juan Gonzalez, *Harvest of Empire: History of Latinos in America* (New York: Penguin Books, 2001); Eduardo Galeano, *Open Veins of Latin America* (New York: NYU Press, 1997).
26. Maribel Santiago and Tadashi Dozono, "History is Critical: Addressing the False Dichotomy Between Historical Inquiry and Criticality," *Theory & Research in Social Education* 50, no. 2, (2022): 173–95, https://doi.org/10.1080/00933104.2022.2048426.
27. Clint Smith, "How Culturally Responsive Lessons Teach Critical Thinking," *Learning for Justice*, November 25, 2019, https://www.learningforjustice.org/magazine/spring-2020/how-culturally-responsive-lessons-teach-critical-thinking.
28. Mayers and Freedman, *Solito, Solita*, 126–29.
29. Mayers and Freedman, *Solito, Solita*, 126.
30. Mayers and Freedman, *Solito, Solita*, 128.

Afterword

1. Michel-Rolph Trouillot, *Silencing the Past: Power and the Production of History* (Boston, MA: Beacon Press, 2015).
2. Resmaa Menakem, *My Grandmother's Hands: Racialized Trauma and the Pathway to Mending Our Hearts and Bodies* (London: Penguin UK, 2021), 4.
3. Shawn Ginwright, *Hope and Healing in Urban Education: How Urban Activists and Teachers Are Reclaiming Matters of the Heart* (New York: Routledge, 2015), 89.

Acknowledgments

The ideas that led to this book began in the summer of 2019 in New York. Doctors Terrie Epstein and LaGarrett King invited us to their conference on Race/Ethnicity and Social Studies. The rich conversations on the place of racial and ethnic knowledge in social studies inspired us to rethink how we frame, acknowledge, and center racial and ethnic community knowledge in the field. For this, we are indebted to Terrie and LaGarrett.

This book would not be possible without the contributors: Meredith, Brittany, Dawnavyn, LaGarrett, Daphanie, Eliana, Krista, Muna, Jocyl, Lauren, Yianella, Mirelsie, and V (Christina). They wrote deeply personal works that moved us. We are also appreciative that they tackled this work during some deeply difficult times. There were times when the world was figuratively and literally burning and yet they still found ways to continue moving forward.

Samantha Weiman was generous enough to proofread all the chapters and make sure we could tame Chicago Manual Style.

The "Go Team" writing group (Rebecca and Casey) offered lots of structure and lots of ears for us to vent.

We would also like to thank the anonymous reviewers who offered their suggestions and kind encouragement.

Our book editor, Molly Cerrone, was incredibly patient with us. From our initial conversation we were upfront about what we wanted this book to be. Molly was understanding and cheered us on in our vision for the book.

Last, but not least, Wayne Journell suggested us to Harvard Education Press. Wayne, thank you for seeing the value of our possible contribution.

—Maribel and Tadashi

Desde muy temprana edad mi familia me enseño que como oaxaqueño/a/es, zapoteco/a/es, y mexicano/a/es nosotros tenemos un conocimiento único. La idea que existe conocimientos de comunidades raciales y étnicas no es algo novedoso para nosotros. Gracias a Marco Polo y Mamá y Papá Santiago por criarme con estas enseñanzas. El compartir estos aprendizajes en este libro es mi forma de agradecer y compartir la sabiduría de mis antepasados (que por cierto, no están pasados si no muy presentes).

—Maribel

I am forever grateful to my family, and my mom in particular, who instilled in me the importance of family history to keep the family stories of Japanese American incarceration alive. My mom was in many ways my most influential history teacher, providing me with an understanding of our family's perseverance in the face of systemic oppression. To know that our ancestors have long struggled against white supremacy propels me toward future systemic change.

—Tadashi

About the Editors

Maribel Santiago is an associate professor of Justice and Teacher Education at the University of Washington and a 2019 National Academy of Education/Spencer Postdoctoral Fellow. She specializes in the production and consumption of Latinx social studies: what students, policymakers, and educators learn about Latinx communities and how they conceptualize Latinx experiences. Her work has been published in *Cognition and Instruction*, *Journal of the Learning Sciences*, *Teachers College Record*, and *Theory & Research in Social Education*.

Tadashi Dozono is an associate professor of History/Social Science Education at California State University Channel Islands. Through cultural studies, ethnic studies, queer theory, and critical theory, Tadashi's research emphasizes accountability toward the experiences of marginalized students by examining the production of knowledge in high school social studies classrooms. He is the author of *Discipline Problems: How Students of Color Trouble Whiteness in Schools* (University of Pennsylvania Press, 2024). His work has been published in *Theory & Research in Social Education*, *Critical Studies in Education*, and *Race Ethnicity and Education*.

About the Editors

About the Contributors

Lauren Arzaga Daus is a PhD student in the Urban Schooling Division at UCLA. Her research focuses on Ethnic studies Teachers of Color, specifically looking at wellness, grief, and radical joy in education. Daus received her BA in Asian American Studies at San Francisco State University, where she learned the significance of Ethnic studies and her identity as a Pinay, especially during her time teaching with Pin@y Educational Partnerships (PEP). She has her MEd and Social Science Teaching Credential from the University of California, Los Angeles (UCLA).

Daphanie Bibbs is a lifelong learner, doctoral student, and Graduate Fellow at the University at Buffalo Center for K–12 Black History and Racial Literacy Education. After spending four years teaching in Missouri, earning a Master of Science degree in Educational Leadership, and serving as the Assistant Director of "I See You!" Teacher of Color Support Network, Daphanie relocated to Chicago to continue her passion for educating youth in low socioeconomic communities. In addition to researching how Black mothers are monitored in schools, she is also interested in investigating the intersection between Black girlhood and Black motherhood.

M. Yianella Blanco is an assistant professor of education at the University of California, Davis. She specializes in the teaching of Latinx histories and experiences in K–12 schooling, particularly those of Central America(ns). Her recent research focuses on the teaching and learning of immigration from the Isthmus and how those intersect with American imperialism and empire. She earned her PhD from Teachers College, Columbia University, and prior to that, she worked as a high school special education and social studies teacher in New York City.

Eliana Castro is an assistant professor of history/social studies education at Boston College. She was born in the Dominican Republic and is the proud descendant of brujas. She studies how history/social studies curricula can promote nuanced representations of intersectional racial/ethnic identities, such as AfroLatinidad. Castro combines teacher and student experiences to probe theories of teaching and learning, racial identity formation, and racial literacy development. Her work has appeared in such peer-reviewed outlets as the *American Educational Research Journal, Journal of Teacher Education, The Social Studies, Teaching and Teacher Education*, and *the Journal of Social Studies Research.*

Krista L. Cortes is the director of La Casa Latina at the University of Pennsylvania. She is a first-generation AfroPuerto Rican mother/scholar/activist who was born and raised in the diaspora. Academically and professionally, Cortes's work is defined by transformative research and practices that uplift people historically oppressed and marginalized in university settings. Considering the politics of place, movement, and the transnational nature of AfroLatinx communities, Cortes's research explores how Blackness is imbued in practices, such as spirituality or hair care, and how Blackness-as-practice is taught and learned.

Dawnavyn James is a PhD student at the University at Buffalo and a fellow at the Center for K–12 Black History and Racial Literacy Education. She is an early childhood, elementary, and Black history educator, and Black history researcher. James is the author of *Beyond February: Teaching Black History Any Day, Every Day, and All Year Long*, which centers her experiences teaching Black histories in elementary classrooms and provides strategies for other educators to do the same.

Brittany Jones is an assistant professor at the University at Buffalo. Informed by her experiences as a social studies teacher, Jones's research explores antiracist social studies teacher education and how racialized emotions inform the teaching and learning of history, with a specific focus on Black emotions. Jones's work also interrogates how race, power, and emotional discourse intersect within social studies standards and curricula. Her work has been published in outlets such as *Theory and Research in Social Education, Equity & Excellence in Education*, and *Education Week.* Jones was also the recipient of the 2023–2024 NCSS Exemplary Research Award.

LaGarrett J. King is an associate professor in the Graduate School of Education at the University at Buffalo and founding director of the Center for K–12 Black

History and Racial Literacy Education. His research focuses on the teaching and learning of Black histories, critical theories of race, and racial literacies. King has won numerous awards and most recently won the Spirit of America Award from NCSS. He has written four books and over sixty articles that have been published in journals such as the *Journal of Negro Education*, *Urban Education*, and *Theory and Research in Social Education*. King also edits a special edition of *Education Week* each Black History Month.

Meredith L. McCoy (Turtle Mountain Ojibwe descent) is an assistant professor of American Studies and History at Carleton College. Her research examines how Indigenous families, educators, and community leaders have long repurposed tools of settler violence into tools for Indigenous life. McCoy has previously worked as a middle school teacher, a Policy Assistant at the White House Initiative on American Indian and Alaska Native Education, and an instructor at Turtle Mountain Community College and Freedom University.

Jocyl Sacramento is an associate professor of Ethnic Studies at California State University, East Bay, where she serves as the Director of Curriculum and Pedagogy for INSPIRE, a First Year Experience program. Her praxis bridges Asian American Studies with Women of Color feminisms, relational racialization, Ethnic studies pedagogies, Pinayism, and love. She coedited the forthcoming Comparative Ethnic Studies textbook *Love, Knowledge, and Revolution* (Routledge). Sacramento completed her MA and PhD in Education from the University of California, Berkeley. She earned her MA in Asian American Studies from SF State, where she taught high school Filipina/x/o American Studies with Pin@y Educational Partnerships.

Muna Saleh is an associate professor of education at Concordia University of Edmonton (CUE), former elementary and secondary school teacher, mother to three awesome humans, and the author of *Stories We Live and Grow By: (Re)Telling Our Experiences as Muslim Mothers and Daughters*. Drawing upon her experiences as an intergenerational survivor of violent Palestinian displacement and as a caregiver to a child with a dis/ability, her most recent research includes narrative inquiries alongside Palestinian Muslim youth and families/caregivers and Muslim mothers of children with dis/abilities who arrived in Canada with refugee experiences.

Index